MY LAST DOOR

ANHINGA PRESS

OTHER BOOKS BY WENDY BISHOP

Keywords in Creative Writing
Co-authored with David Starkey, Utah State University Press, 2004

Thirteen Ways of Looking for a Poem: A Guide to Writing Poetry
Longman, 2000

When We Say We're Home: A Quartet of Place and Memory
with W. Scott Olsen, Dawn Murano, and Douglas Carlson
University of Utah Press, 1999

Released into Language:
Options for Teaching Creative Writing, Second Edition
Calendar Islands Press, 1998

Working Words: The Process of Creative Writing
Mayfield Publishing Co., 1992

POETRY CHAPBOOKS

Mid-Passage
Nightshade Press, 1998
1997 Winner of the William and Kingman Page Chapbook Award

Touching Liliana
Jumping Cholla Press, 1998

My 47 Lives
Palanquin Press, 1998
1998 Winner of the Palanquin Press Poetry Chapbook Contest

Water's Night
Co-authored with Hans Ostrom, Maraposite Press, 1992

Second Nature
Tideline Press, 1980

MY LAST DOOR

WENDY BISHOP

POEMS

ANHINGA PRESS
TALLAHASSEE, FLORIDA
2007

Copyright © Dean Newman 2007
All rights reserved under
International and Pan-American Copyright Conventions.

No portion of this book may be reproduced in any form without the written permission of the publisher, except by a reviewer, who may quote brief passages in connection with a review for a magazine or newspaper.

Cover art: *Wendy's Quilt*, quilt by Linda Hall (photograph by Jon Nalon)
Author photo: Tait Pollard
Cover design, book design, and production: C. L. Knight
Typesetting: Jill Ihasz
Type Styles: titles set in Lithos Pro and text set in Novarese

Library of Congress Cataloging-in-Publication Data
My Last Door by Wendy Bishop – First Edition
ISBN – 978-0-938078-96-8
Library of Congress Cataloging Card Number – 2007922816

This publication is sponsored in part by a grant
from the Florida Department of State,
Division of Cultural Affairs, and the Florida Arts Council.

Anhinga Press Inc. is a nonprofit corporation dedicated wholly to the
publication and appreciation of fine poetry and other literary genres.

For personal orders, catalogs
and information write to:
Anhinga Press
P.O. Box 10595
Tallahassee, Florida 32302
Web site: www.anhinga.org
E-mail: info@anhinga.org

Published in the United States
by Anhinga Press
Tallahassee, Florida

811.54 BIS
2002 5691 03-15-21 NEB
Bishop, Wendy, 1953-2003.

My last door
jmf

For Wendy

Love, Dean, Morgan, and Tait
and hundreds of others who loved her, too.

Cover Art
Wendy's Quilt,
by Linda Hall
4' X 5 1/2', hand-dyed fabric
piecework, embroidery thread,
and glass beads.

This piece was inspired by a window on the Gulf of Mexico at Wendy and Dean's Alligator Point home at dusk, the magic hour that Wendy loved when the sky and the water became the same color. The birds with human heads come from the ancient Egyptian Ba-Bird, the vehicle through which the deceased can move in and out of the tomb, between life and the "eternal house."
— Linda Hall

CONTENTS

xiii   Acknowledgments
xvii   Introduction

1. THE POEM YOU ASKED FOR

- 3   Everything
- 5   The Poem You Asked For
- 6   Tradition and the Individual Talents
- 8   Ordinary Language Philosophy: A Sestina Plus One Line
- 10   Pantoum on Lines by Wallace Stegner
- 12   A Man and a Woman Are Not an Island
- 13   Rainbow Bridge
- 15   Valentines: A Pantoum Using Lines from My Other Poems
- 16   How Not to Write
- 18   Blue Lovers
- 21   The Words We've Worked with This Week
- 23   The Sculptor's House
- 25   How Does a Poem Start?
- 26   Roland Barthes on E-mail
- 27   A New Poem about Old Losses
- 28   A Short Course in the Sonnet
- 29   The Southwest: O'Keeffe and Steiglitz
- 30   Inside Out
- 32   Fool for Doubles
- 33   The Rocking Chair, Again
- 34   In Medias Res

II. THE LIGHT AT THE END OF THE YEAR

- 39   North Florida Nocturne
- 40   On Passions
- 41   Without Oceans
- 42   My Vision, One Saturday in March
- 43   Grayton Beach
- 45   Gardenia

46	Report
47	Prescription for Winter
48	How to Be a Shell
49	Terzanelle on Drought
50	If Over Your Shoulder the Hangnail Moon
51	To Get Rain
52	Another Celestial Circuit in North Florida
53	Back Corners
54	The Farm
55	To Seed
57	Thursday's Weather
59	Of Summer
60	Approaching Ennui
61	On Giving and Finding Gifts
62	Call Me Ishmael
64	From a Bottle
65	My Armadillo
66	Coastal
67	Wishing Spring: A Ghazal
68	The Summer Season
70	The Light at the End of the Year
71	Gulf Shells
72	Where the Hummingbird Sips, There Sip I: An Appreciation
75	Centers of Gravity

III. THE NEW WORLD

79	Journey
80	The New World
82	Hills
84	Dawn Song
86	The Ice Palace
88	Garden

91	The Brickmaker's Sinkhole at Goron Dutse, Nigeria
93	Blue Moon I: An Elegy
96	Lovers and Tribes
98	Diary, Photographer, 1850: The Yucatan
100	Lindberg Comes to Canyon de Chelly
102	Your Apple Tree
104	Return to Oaxaca
105	Gypsy Dance in Progress in a Sunlit Corner of a Courtyard of Southern Serbia
106	Grass: A Museum
108	1225 B.C.
110	Awake Early on Todos Santos
111	Angels on the Amazon
112	The Distance to Rhodes
113	Cache Creek
114	Chichicastenango
115	Findings on the Underground
116	On the Chihuahua-Pacifico Railway
117	Archeologist's Widow

IV. TO GO HOME

121	The Peace in Peace: An Epithalemion
122	In Summer
123	In Your Childhood Bedroom
126	The Way I Remember
128	Slight Archaic
130	How One May Morning Leads to Another
132	My Children Help Me Cut My Hair
134	First Marriage
135	When You Drive Away
137	Omnivores
139	The Divorce Quilt
140	Sestina: on What They Remember

142	Why Men Snore
144	Men Who Leave
145	Men Who Travel Toward Themselves
147	Later in Life
148	Black Sheep
149	Gillian Alone
151	Why Sing of a Father Unathletic
152	To Start My Father's Heart
153	House/Home
156	Fever Bouquet
157	For My Daughter on Her Glasses
158	The Density of White
159	In the Wedding Barn
161	At Eighteen
162	Storm
164	On Shelters
165	Moors and Christians — A Sestina
167	Here in the New World
168	IQ and Age
169	A Teacher Myself, I Consider My Children's Schools
171	House Building
173	Early Morning Muse
174	Self-Portrait: Tait
175	Preteen
176	To Go Home
179	Relatives Relatives
181	Autobiography

V. OUR SHORT GREEN LIVES

185	The Cultivation of Mind
186	The Red Clearing
187	Mid-Passage
188	Brain Tectonics

190	Inland Seas
192	Rage and Gratitude Are Hunger's Angels
194	In My Cups
197	The Other One
199	Part of Things
200	A Heart with Eyes, an Empty Dress, a Boat Made of Dirt
201	My Religious Development: A Paradelle for Jeremy
202	A Short Introduction to Phobias
204	The Shamans
206	Glass Houses
207	Ghosts' Story
208	Three P.M.
209	Frankenstein
211	Fortune
212	Addressing the Body
213	After Epiphany
214	Teaching the Trick New Dogs: A Phrenologist Dreams
216	Death
218	Clothes Closet
219	The First Man
220	Water's Night
221	My Last Door
223	Coming Back
224	On Orange
225	Othering
227	The Cancer Patient Writes in the Dark
229	This Time
231	Skating and Sleighing to the Icy Vaults of Death
232	My Impatience
233	I Learn to Stand Up Straight
235	Dreams of Houses
237	About the Author

ACKNOWLEDGMENTS

Grateful acknowledgment to the publications in which these poems first appeared:

"1225 B.C." *Cutbank*, 1976

"A Man and a Woman Are Not an Island," *College English*, 1989

"Addressing the Body," *Poetry Northwest*, 1983

"After Epiphany," *Harvest*, 1978

"Angels on the Amazon," *Rhino*, 1990

"Another Celestial Circuit in North Florida," *Mischief, Caprice, and Other Poetic Strategies*, Red Hen Press, and *The Ohio Poetry Review*, 1995

"Archeologist's Widow," *Heartland*, 1986, and *Slant* 6, 1992

"Autobiography," 5 AM, Issue #10

"Brain Tectonics," *Cottonwood Review*, 1992

"Cache Creek," *Fresh Water: Poems from the Rivers, Lakes, and Streams*, Pudding House Press, 2003

"Centers of Gravity," *High Plains Literary Review*, 1991

"Chichicastenango," *English Journal*, 1989

"Clothes Closet," *Wisconsin Review*, 1995

"Coming Back," *Rockhurst Review 2000: A Fine Arts Journal*, 2000

"Diary, Photographer, 1850: The Yucatan," *Northwest Review*, 1980

"Diary, Photographer, 1850: The Yucatan," "Dawn Song: Capay Valley," "Addressing the Body," and "If Over Your Shoulder the Hangnail Moon," *Golddust*, 1986

"Everything," *The MacGuffin*, 2003

"Everything," "My Children Help Me Cut My Hair," "In Your Childhood Bedroom," "Inside Out," "Valentines: A Pantoum Using Lines from My Other Poems," "The Peace in Peace: An Epithalemion," *River Oak Review*, 2004

"Fever Bouquet," *Food Poems*, Bottom Dog Press, 2003

"Findings on the Underground," *The Poetry Miscellany*, 1982

"First Marriage," *Prairie Schooner*, 1987

"Frankenstein," and "The Summer Season," *The Windless Orchard*, 1978-1979, and Calendar insert

"From a Bottle," *Glassworks: An Anthology of Poems and Stories*, Pudding House, 2003

"Garden," *Louisville Review*, 1983

"Gardenia," *The Georgia Review*, 1998

"Gillian Alone," *Quarter After Eight*, 1997

"Grass: A Museum," *Brahma*, 1978, *Valley Light: Writers of the San Joaquin*, Poets and Printers Press, 1978, and *So Luminous the Wildflowers: Anthology of California Poets*, Tebot Bach, 2003

"Gypsy Dance in Progress," *Mississippi Review*, 1983 and *Northwest Poets and Artists Calendar*, 1988

"Here in the New World," *The Higgensville Reader*, 2000

"How One May Morning Leads to Another," *Hawaii Pacific Review*, 1999

"If Over Your Shoulder the Hangnail Moon," and "Cache Creek," *Prairie Schooner*, 1985

"If Over Your Shoulder the Hangnail Moon," *The Archer*, 1986/1987

"In Summer," *Heartland – Fairbanks Daily News Miner*, 1988, and *The Green Mountain Review*, 1990

"Moors and Christians — A Sestina," *Troubadour: A Journal of Lyric Poetry*, 1999

"My Last Door," *Bayou: A Journal of Poetry & Prose*, 2002

"Omnivores," *Palanquin Press Pamphlet Series*, 1997

"On Giving and Finding Gifts," *Eclipse*, 2003

"On Orange," *Natural Bridges*, 2002

"On Passions," *Black Water Review*, 1999

"On Shelters," *Rhino*

"On the Chihuahua-Pacifico Railway," *River City*, 1990

"Ordinary Language Philosophy: A Sestina Plus One Line,"
     "Wishing Spring: A Ghazal," and "Pantoum on Lines
     by Wallace Stegner," *The Rio Grande Review.*

"Othering," *Seneca Review*

"Part of Things," *Buffalo Carp*, 2002

"Prescription for Winter," *University of Windsor Review*, 1989

"Return to Oaxaca," *College Composition and Communication*, 1992

"Roland Barthes on E-mail," and "Fool for Doubles," in *King Log*
     (on-line journal. http://www.angelfire.com/il/kinglog)

"Slight Archaic," *Classical Outlook*, 1985

"Terzanelle on Drought," *Alligator Juniper*, 1996

"The Brickmakers' Sinkhole at Goron Dutse," *Heartland*, 1986

"The Cultivation of Mind," *Prairie Schooner*, 1992

"The Density of White," and "The Cancer Victim Writes in the Dark,"
     The Berkeley Poetry Review, 1976.

"The Distance to Rhodes," *Wind/Literary Journal*, 1980

"The Divorce Quilt," *Heartland*, 1986

"The Farm," *Santa Clara Review*, 1994

"The First Man," *Poetry Now*, 1980

"The Light at the End of the Year," *Heartland*, 1985, and *Poem*, 1987

"The Other One," *Permafrost*, 1986

"The Red Clearing," *Defined Providence*

"The Shamans," *Silverfish Review*, 1979

"The Southwest: O'Keeffe and Stieglitz," *The Southwest Review*, 1986

"The Way I Remember," *SunDog*, 1996

"To Start My Father's Heart," *College English*, 1994.

"Water's Night," *Bellingham Review*, 1979

"Why Sing of a Father Unathletic," *Kansas Quarterly*, 1987

"Without Oceans," *The Iowa Review*, 2002

"Your Apple Tree," *Denver Quarterly*, 1986

INTRODUCTION

by Katharine Haake

Wendy Bishop was among my closest friends for a full quarter century, and though we never lived near enough to meet for coffee or, another favorite, martinis, or to help each other out with our kids, or share the mundane detritus of daily life, our intimacies spanned the country through the round middle parts of our lives and took the form, always, of writing. When we met at the first Santa Cruz Writer's Conference in 1978, Wendy was the full scholarship poet and I, the half scholarship fiction writer. The conference lasted two weeks, and for the first, we eyed each other warily — I, drawn to Wendy, like everyone else, for her passion, her beauty, her amazing presence in language, and I remember being stunned when she finally overcame whatever shyness lay between us and turned her full attention on me. This happened in a meadow on a hill below campus, the sparkling blue Monterey Bay stretched out below, and Wendy was surrounded, as always at that time, by a gaggle of admiring guys. I remember, too, her wide open laughter, the astonishing reds in her trademark long auburn hair, the folds of her paisley skirt dangling just above her beautiful feet. I don't know what she said or did to part the guys and draw me in to her most intimate circle, but in my memory it remains as one of those singular moments in life when everything changes in a heartbeat, and it was the start of a great and lasting friendship and an altered life in language. People who knew Wendy will understand when I say writing was about to shift for me from something I'd been doing for several years by then, a purpose, maybe, and what felt like a vocation, to a whole entire way of life. What I learned from Wendy over the years was that writing is not something one does, but a way someone lives — acutely, perpetually present and observant in language.

Wendy's poems are an expression of that way of life, and she never met a moment she could not turn into a poem. After the manner of Italo Calvino, her work is quick and light, modeling for the rest of us a way of being in words that would sustain itself because it was as vital as it was necessary. Throughout the years I knew her, Wendy made a daily practice of writing, and I remember one summer morning when we were vacationing in my family cabin in northern California. The kids were in their shrieking kickball kid part of their growing up and we'd been up late, as usual, talking writing and life, but when I stumbled out at 8:00 to make the coffee, I was only half surprised to find it brewed already, Wendy at work in the kitchen in a light gray sweatshirt, editing a massive composition volume she'd brought cross country with her. I expect she'd been at it for hours already, but before that day was out, she'd have made another poem or another poem would have begun to make itself in her.

   This book collects a sampling of those poems, a monumental record that is long overdue. For despite her bright beginnings — among all of us at Santa Cruz, she was widely acknowledged as the one who was going to "make it;" and her graduate school teachers were predicting a book within the year, prizes, recognitions, a life on the poetry circuit — among the more than twenty books on writing she did publish in her lifetime, this is her first full book of poems. Culled from a welter of manuscripts and computer files by the painstaking and devoted attentions of Wendy's husband, Dean Newman, and her colleagues in teaching and poetry itself, Laura Newton and Jane Springer, it is divided into five fungible parts, organized, in this order, around: writing, the natural world, place, family, death. But as Laura herself somewhat wryly observes, though each poem fits into its appointed section, it could just as easily go into another, and like a complex math equation, confound us with its variability. Poems of place for Wendy are often poems of home; poems of family are poems of place as well; and every poem takes writing at the core.

Geologist, biologist, botanist, observer of flora and fauna and shoulder of hill, mother, lover, daughter, friend — Wendy took up any stance she could to map in poetry a life lived out in the paradoxical struggle for peace of the restless and passionate mind. An insatiable traveler when I first met her and a wanderer by nature, Wendy paced an exotic path back and forth across two continents and several marriages before, finally, geography stopped her and she finally came to rest in the far southeast corner of this country, jammed up against the wrong gulf, which over time, she would make her own. "It's not bad for a foreign posting," she used to say of Florida, to which she had driven in a U-Haul from Alaska, where she had driven, in another U-Haul, from the Navajo Reservation in Arizona, where she had landed by way of Nigeria, from California, both northern and southern. Here, the wonders of family and work, the daily miracles of raising children and teaching writing and revising entire academic disciplines and building homes and taking stock took up the attention and energy with which she had once embraced the wider world. As a poet, she recast the same observant eye she'd once turned to love and whale, to rock and bat and flaming skies, to hold the mysteries of her family, home, and back yard. Fiercely devoted to her children and determined to take them as poetic subject, despite still widely held proscriptions against doing so, when she held them in a poem, it was with the same sense of wonder and keen intelligence she used to hold "crumbling/rock and blue clay," "the ocean you carry within," and sleep "the color of water" — though, like children themselves, they are frequently surprising and funny.

    All the while, Wendy was moving through her life like a keen-eyed archaeologist, stripping away at the surface of things in search of the poem at the core, not as artifact but as trace, remnant of living thing — of moments lived. She made her poems like offerings, and like offerings, left them easily behind, always interested more in the next one that was coming than in the ones that came before, despite her other writerly preoccupations with memory and writing both. For Wendy loved not just the world and our life in it, but the way language worked, felt, moved, was. And she loved, as well, the play of form and what it could release for writer, reader, poem. If a poetic form exists, and even if it doesn't, you will find it in this book. From sonnet to pantoum to the farce of paradelle, Wendy saw each tradition and constraint as an occasion for both writing and surprise.

The poems that make the latter part of this book may be seen as remarkable for their preoccupations with death, may feel eerily prescient. She was a young and vital woman — what might account for this wary awareness of things perpetually ending? Wendy lost her father when she was still an adolescent; she lost her mother shortly before she had her first child. These biographical details may seem to explain her poems about death, but I think their origins are plainer than that. For just as Wendy could not look at a fitch or a soccer ball or haircut assisted by children without recognizing the presence of a poem, she could not experience that presence without being equally attuned, not to its absence, but to its transience. These poems mark life, they also mark time, and marking time, mark, exquisitely, loss. It wasn't going to last, she knew. None of it would last. Better than the rest of us, Wendy knew this all along. So she took each moment and lived it with a passion verging on ferocity, and every moment that she could, she turned permanent in words.

Once again," she writes in "On Orange," "I think. Let sun's nectar, time's sharp juice/pulse down my throat. Don't let me forget." The book begins, "I want to be the word under your tongue,/and the tongue that finds that word, and it ends:

> Memories can so fill a place
> They are slow to disperse.
> The house, though changed, waits for me
> Whenever I return at night to rest.
> So I closed the door before I left.

We are the places that Wendy fills now, and the door that is closed lies waiting for us. This book, long overdue, contains her memories, to which we can return now, over and over, like Wendy, to rest — and go on.

> Often only in imagination.
> To be reborn.
> Stepping into the next story,
> just after the next story unfolds.
> — In Media Res

MY LAST DOOR

I. THE POEM YOU ASKED FOR

EVERYTHING

> *Every contact, for the lover, raises the question of an answer ...*
> — Roland Barthes

I want to be the word under your tongue,
and the tongue that finds that word,
in the all-day hotel room; the light
that slips across a tossed bed
the way a leg slips across another leg.
I plan to build a sentence
like a chain — the valuable kind
tasteless men wear
to underline shirts open to the waist.
I want to spend time stringing words
into your inner ear,
drop memories like Psyche's
candle wax onto dreams, wake you up surprised,
at 3 a.m., into another dream. I will
indent each paragraph on my knees,
find the right length and heft,
the sweet and salt of punctuation and precision,
that means, mostly, eyes closed and go ahead.
I look ahead to the next page, the new leaf,
leap over an obstructing stream, and walk on
to a beach, lie arms outstretched,
reading this instant, cover to cover.
I want to store pages in your eyes,
rewrite them before they reach
fingertips. I find your fingers
hard to type. I type these wishes
on the closed book of your back,
decide to believe that

even if there are only seven basic plots
all of them are possible. I want
to stand face to face,
exchange the first word
for this
the next first word.

THE POEM YOU ASKED FOR

is sharp. An oboe reed in my throat,
it vibrates when I breathe
and when I sleep, it tries to sleep.

The poem you thought I might write,
is bone-fine and thin-skinned,
a white china bowl on a high kitchen shelf
I can never quite reach.

You have not read this poem —
a spider washed down the drain
while you thought of other things.
Part of the poem is your name

on the lips of a child
who still waits. This poem like a thread
on my shoulder, you dare not remove
and dare not leave alone.

The poem you thought I would send
floated along rivers for weeks,
reflected the skies and then sank
to the far shores of sight.

I've written the poem so often;
it marks time, unfolds like crushed paper
in a young cat's claws,
as she sleeps and forgets to play.

Years ago, the poem
you expected walked out —
but continues to travel toward us
ever since you first asked it to arrive.

TRADITION AND THE INDIVIDUAL TALENTS

Inevitably, all students of poetry
write drugs

while aiming for their fix of holy fire,
so I scramble the letters, and add to them —

rugs and *shrugs* and *dugs* and *drudge* —
to show how much words may mean,

how stories
can be unpacked and repacked

in a detonation
of connotation,

suggest that *fuckguitar*
is somewhere all of us have been —

heads dizzied down on a rough wooden counter —
that's why the older poets placed themselves

ritually in ovens
and institutions,

because the life of the mind will always find escape
as poetry goes urgently into each bad night

of orchestrated readings
and correctly angled beer mugs,

while the middle aged move
from *aspirin* through *xanax*,

collect wine-rich Rivieras,
compile verse about

paintings and saints fading
from the walls of history,

compound their interest
in *been theres, done thats*,

when it's word mantras that matter —
gush shred drags dodge.

In the rich silences
between rhyme and free, a faraway look

on each generational face.

ORDINARY LANGUAGE PHILOSOPHY: A SESTINA PLUS ONE LINE

for Tom O'Donnell — rhetorical philosopher

> *But, with some unimportant reservations, it is true to say that coins, checks, stamps, separate words, buttons and shoelaces offer no scope for talent. Either a person knows or he does not know how to use and how not to misuse them.*
> — Gilbert Ryle.

My father knew how to use coins.
We'd check bags of new nickels
for mis-stamps, like E *Pluribus Unum*
written as one, not separate words,
save the good bad ones, round as buttons,
in a handkerchief tied with his shoelace.

My son hates tying his shoelaces,
but has mastered the math of coins.
He struggles with the top shirt button
or misbuttons all in haste, I check him, tidy
up, he barks out his words — *thank — you —*
and stamps out to the school bus stop.

I stamp another letter. Tie my
shoelace by the mailbox where my words
wait for delivery under the Spanish dagger.
Blooms like white coins flourish
and fade before I check the next day:
browned fallen buttons on the ground.

When my mother died, I took old buttons
from a small tin box, some stamped, some
embossed, checked the closet twice —

bargain coats and shoes, few with laces —
from kitchen drawers emptied coins,
lint, a note with her final words.

I separate words, those I use easily
and those I button inside. Like a counter-
feiter, coin what I can for what I need:
here's a mouth and tongue to stamp
what I say, to lace my meaning into air.
Is what I say, what I mean? I'll check.

But to check, I must interrogate,
case by case. I separate words into piles
like my children's broken shoelaces,
missing buttons (and the extras a good
shirt supplies). Satisfied, I stamp the day
correct, coin the unusual on my own time.

Everyone knows, coins are not checks
and words don't fly without their stamps.
If he doesn't know not to button his shoelaces:
he must have talent, he is not ordinary.

PANTOUM ON LINES BY WALLACE STEGNER

Like raw earth and alkali flats,
sagebrush is an acquired taste.
The west is less a person
than a continuing adaptation.

Sagebrush is an acquired taste.
I miss the sight of bare ground
and the continuing adaptation
of earth colors — tan, rusty, red.

I miss the sight of bare ground
bits of east, middle west, are buried here
in earth. Colored tan, rusty, red,
I'm used to sunrise over mountains.

Bits of east, middle west, are buried here
but west is never found in the east.
I'm used to sunrise over mountains
and sunset over other mountains.

West is never found in the east.
It's less a place than a process
like sun setting over mountains.
Western culture, automobiles, motels.

It's less a place than a process.
The endless greens of Iowa offended me.
Western culture, automobiles, motels,
to live in and be shaped by bigness.

The endless greens of Iowa offended me.
I missed the color and smell of sagebrush.

Living in and shaped by bigness
I was used to horizons, jagged ranges.

I missed the color and smell of sagebrush.
Like I missed the west, like a person
of wide horizons, jagged ranges,
acquired taste of raw earth and alkali flats.

A MAN AND A WOMAN
ARE NOT AN ISLAND

Neither are they a boat, an octopus, or a torpedo.

Coming out of water, they are not a steam engine,
  a melting popsicle, a lung.

If anything, they imitate metallic
  ether when lightning flashes through,
  the jet airplane diving at your spine,
  the sullen breath of an all day rainstorm.

She is not his housekeeper and he is not her hero
  although they both feel something for the mortgage.

He is not his father and she is not her mother
  although they are the spitting image of their children.

Moving into night, he is not her story and she is not
  his radio. They are not an argument or artichoke,
  a means or way. They are not Sputniks or footrubs.

If anything, they understand individual Esperanto.
  If anything, they agree on chimneys and adultery
  but not under freeways.

A man and a woman are not an island. If lucky,
  they may be their own day. If unlucky,
  they may have to be an island.

RAINBOW BRIDGE

Leaving my forties,
I leave backpacking behind,
leave three days on the Inca Trail,
Dead Woman's pass,
mountainsides filling my boots
with dry gray dirt clods.
I sidestep the steep funneling
slide down into Machu Picchu,
the high altitude headaches
and wonder. I am no longer
three months pregnant,
determined to address the world,
by sticking my knife blades
between building blocks —
one last time.

Leaving my forties.
I leave backpacking behind,
its promising weight and song:
"House on my back, oh, house on my back!"
Rigorous cinching down
of padded hip-belt; bloom of bruises
on hipbones, certain pride
at swinging heavy pack off alone.
I leave the ledge without resting there
trembling, relaxed, sips of flat water,
tongue rasp of hard red candies
votive offerings to spit;
I leave bumblebees
suspended in bright air
above a switchback trail
that arrives, another day's hike,
at Rainbow Bridge, its rock arch.

Leaving my forties,
I leave backpacking behind,
turn my back on Edward Weston rocks,
sandstone hummocks, rainwater pools,
flowering cottonwood, green and rare,
scatter of pollens sailing
across the narrow canyon
on dusty handfuls of afternoon sunlight.
How quietly it happens.
I stop practicing for Peru.
I set aside Indian country.
I give away backpack,
I file away words, I describe.

VALENTINES: A PANTOUM
USING LINES FROM MY OTHER POEMS

The moon brushes the shallows of my back.
Not a day passed, I didn't want you.
You were the full shoulder, the dependable door.
I work at my desk then move through the rooms.

Not a day passed, I didn't want you.
My body changes with seasons, with moons.
I work at my desk then move through the rooms.
I might have mentioned the wonder of mouths.

My body changes with seasons, with moons.
You take things as you find them.
I might have mentioned the wonder of mouths.
My fingers feather your wrist in the quiet after work.

You take things as you find them.
You are the full shoulder, the dependable door.
My fingers feather your wrist in the quiet after work
The moon brushes the shallows of my back.

HOW NOT TO WRITE

Not an inch of poetry in this day.
I listen to the unlooked for emptiness,

to the wide bright sweep of all windows open
first time this late-summer-not-quite-autumn,

to the random dance of barely moving
Chinese maples (considering which

leaves will fall first?) and the brush of lovebugs
on the wirescreens (as I imagine them) moving

all night until they fall to windowsill dust
that I might clean out in the cicada sunlight

of an unexpectedly unhumid morning.
How to spend it? Like unwinding a silkworm.

Unsure of direction. Even over a familiar bowl of cereal.
A morning when neighbors not seen all summer

beyond the back fence begin to gnaw
with a chainsaw at last spring's fallen oak.

Cabbage palms have grown into their places,
strain the slight rising breeze into green spiny light

that falls through windows. The house
glows like a geode. It's a gift of a day,

unpoetically simple, hours drifting across
ceiling fans, kids invited to neighbors'

houses, leaving snail tracks of occupancy
but none of the slamming and banging fanfares,

arias of FM and AM, rancor from dark rooms.
Just three-fourths of a grilled cheese sandwich

left on the counter, speaks of satiety, and this peace.

BLUE LOVERS

*And there's something to be said for fucking up. In fact, fucking up,
if you aspire to be an artist, may be the great creative principle: getting
broken, broken wide open, and then delving among the shards.*
— Breyten Breytenbach

no artist, but i've had my day
fucking up —
when i drove the car straight

into the telephone pole, making my
sixteen year old's
bad turn behind the grocery store.

or that trip alone to europe, 36
hours of proud
travel alone, backpack stolen

from my first night's bed as i slept.
i fucked up
when i decided to live alone

about like i did when i lived together
i have lots
of friends who fuck up,

riding bicycles into moving trucks,
taking up concert
viola at age 33, believing there's something

special about living in the woods
about living
in new york city about what's on tv.

there's nothing like cooking to make you
fuck up — 26 spices
for curry that only get used that once

or like gift-giving, deciding to only give
others what you
want yourself — zebra print skirt, tire-irons.

it's easy to think the government
fucked up again —
treaties, and grain, inoculations and guns.

the people who make my clothes
often fuck up
and charge me a lot for it. it's clear

my parents fucked up, or fucked
somewhat, and thinking
about them, and it, i don't blame them

there's almost more fucking up in love
than lovers to do it
though we're sure we are the exceptions.

etc. etc. there's something romantic
about a person
who gives him or herself to it:

cliff's edge, work for the poor, don't
try to publish the first
six novels, the painting that will finally

feed the family. even honorable people fuck up,
arrested for aiding
and abetting, 16 years in prison for not believing

or for speaking, or for breathing or for
etc. etc.
the world's fucked up, yet we keep meeting:

i'll remember always, each window
i looked out of
talking to you, broken wide open

and right now i can't say whether i've
fucked up again
or have simply earned these shards.

THE WORDS WE'VE WORKED WITH THIS WEEK

include soffit and drywall; a grey ointment
called Noalox that keeps lightbulb ends
from freezing up in sockets (the electrician left it,
his fingerprints in whorls on the plastic bottle);

dollies and a Johnny Lift on the delivery truck,
vinyl trim like confetti on sand-spur beach grass
alongside concrete bits, chunked out with the old
louvered windows, one pane shattered

into summer knives across the back floor
as the last of the wooden porch screens rip
on passing ladders of 6, 8, or 12 feet. We've
picked up lampshade finials, wrenches, stacked

assorted trim, shoved a Plebe toilet bowl from one
spot to the next, waiting for the right-sized
bolt-hole drill-bit. Whirlpool, Asko, Hunter, Amana,
plastic brandnames in bas-relief may survive

salt-filled sea air. Caulk's useful, covers inevitable gaps —
between wall and window, tile and corner — its mending
ability required, for old cinder block resists
new ideas. Electrical and phone cords in conduits —

construction's very own varicose veins. Work by
Fred, Ron, Doug, Ben, by long-haired Jesse, by greyhound
sinewed, molasses-tanned Billy, speckled with paint
and drywall dust; their labor receipts on lined notebook

paper when anyone locates a leaky Bic. GFIC receptacles —
what we don't now know about hardware stores
we don't need to know — couplers and swivels, baffles,
plumber's putty, vents and fans, rings and sleeves,

so many words for fitting in and shaping up, primer
to pilot light, standing seam to serendipity. Consider
how one person passes us on to the next: "Call
Prescott's," "Call Jimmy." One job is well done

another done — just barely — so Friday night's pay is earned.
Gatorade left on a sill; sunset out a well-shimmed
window. It's hard to put down roots in sand, but with
these words, we work to believe that we can.

THE SCULPTOR'S HOUSE

for Ed and Monifa

The sculptor's house resembles
the brain of the sculptor
who sends fire across metal,
shears iron into filigrees of thought.
The sculptor's brain resembles
the house: from dew-rich figures
beyond the backyard window
to flame-painted steel interiors
forged from a junkyard of luck and skill —
malleable and resistant.

He animates at a molecular level.
Ideas circulate:
arc, torque, tension.
Liquid and solid wrestle
as the fiery fuel-line hisses
into further richness
and the intellect sends
its furious tang of sparks into the air.

The sculptor's partner
moves around the chess pieces
of such intentions,
lays her spine of finest alloy
from front door to back porch,
from catalogs to sketchbooks,
for there are rooms and more rooms,
and space requires her clear attention.

The roof provides a skull;
rich as brushstrokes,

welded seams whisper,
shiver up and down the walls.
Hieroglyphic, the front yard mixes
elements like passions — mineral,
vegetable, and animal — animate and still —
rust and patina, thrust of metal — expectant, rampant
and delicate
as the singing bowl inside upon the table,
as the cup of tea's inner flame. The house broods
on its works, and work provides this silence.

HOW DOES A POEM START?

At the beginning of each picture there is someone who works with me. Toward the end I have the impression of having worked without a collaborator.
      — Christian Zervos
         conversation with Picasso in *The Creative Process*.

I thought I saw you
over my left shoulder,
out the study window,
down the centipede grass lawn,
just brushed on the forehead
by the cabbage palm fronds.
As I counted out syllables
on my lips, I was sure your lips
moved. You waved, as I turned
a line, enjambed myself
into the evening.
For I can sit working
as long as the city sleeps
and stars float
like separate spy holes
in the sky's humidity.
Deciding there is a door
for each star.
I open each
to see what is really
just outside this picture.
And only after such euphoria,
do I notice that you are gone.

ROLAND BARTHES ON E-MAIL

As if I have words instead of fingers,
I fall in love with a sentence
spoken to me. I begin to understand.
Language is a skin. Skin replies.

I fall in love with a sentence.
I ask why? I ask when this began,
language as a skin? Skin replies.
I travel a distance, chance a word.

I ask why? I ask when this began.
Spoken to, I begin to understand,
travel a distance, chance a word, as if
I have fingers at the tips of my words.

A NEW POEM ABOUT OLD LOSSES

a word is elegy to what it signifies
— Robert Hass, *Meditation at Lagunitas*

Every word has its own past,
and many forked places, turnings taken
then abandoned for others more tempting.
Once, child meant me, in an elbow of a tinder-
brown hillside with a book, drifting yet anchored
above my parents' house and arguments — meant
not owning myself — meant being older but acting
childish when a callow lover slipped away or when
my father failed. Cancer was a word that scared
my step-mother into stories — she shared hers
with a good friend who said she, too, was afraid —
to make love, at what her husband's wild cells might do,
so they didn't, raised children and cats, waited.
I've lost cats to the tune of seventy lives —
a constellation of lithe, indifferent bodies
precedes me into a cryptic darkness —
but today, my green-eyed one has returned.
His slipped lost-collar found, we scooped him,
chirruping, from a neighbor's doorstep.
He gets amnesia without his tags which, resumed,
change him back into a housecat, whimpering
lost dreams into new sleep. See — I've only
traced the edges of the letter C — child,
cancer, cat; callow, cell, cryptic; constellation,
collar, chirrup, change — I've only started —
but I have lived long enough to know that every past
has its own words, welcomes its own elegy.
Here's enough work, then, for my small eternity:
I set out dictionaries on the hard wood floor —
resume my diligent earthly study.

A SHORT COURSE IN THE SONNET

In English it's divided into three
Sicilian quatrains and one heroic
couplet; twelve lines and then a turn is needed
to emphasize the climax and the subject.

The Italian has an eight and a six:
more rhymes repeat, the turn of thought takes place
sooner: less time to explain, more to fix
the return. Syllabic lines; accent racing,

pentameter heartbeats: ta-DUM, times five.
To simplify, let's call it ten by fourteen.
The prosody handbook proclaims new kinds
develop weekly, words propagating.

A novice taps Morse Code, chants: abab
bcbc cdcd ee?

THE SOUTHWEST: O'KEEFFE AND STEIGLITZ

She stands in the sunlight
That shapes her in the doorway,
Timbers and adobe,
Shadows as rich as those
At her breasts and eyelids,
Shadows like the rough scrawl of charcoal
Or the dark cloth over his head
As he centers in the viewfinder
Her lips
Curved to match the tension of his hands.

She remembers walking one dawn
In a gray light, in an endless length
Of open landscape, dirt and desiccated bone:
The rising sun turning red beyond all reds
And fleshing out her face.

He wasn't present
Yet his photographs show it.
His genius, to know her as his mate,
Even at a distance.
And now they move into the house,
Damn the guests!
They lived a moment
And gave away what was left
In the enigmatic silver of his prints.

INSIDE OUT

Today I blazed through town —
my pastel-striped V-neck T-shirt worn
inside out. Neck tags covered by Cinnaberry-red
hastily washed hair, seams showing around
the shoulders and down my yellow-aqua-coral-dun striped sides.

At the Animal Aid Clinic, no one noticed. Dogs
attended to their own bristly business; cats moaned
from a line of plastic pet taxis, and stared malevolently
clear through me. Picking up mail from the office mailroom, why,
I felt no wilder than usual. A student looked sideways at her tatter
of bulletin board notices. The receptionist made small talk
about travel and weather, neglected to say: "Dr. Bishop ... about
your shirt." Sunglasses misplaced already that morning,
I knew my head wasn't on right. Because I live inside that head,
and not in the mirror's glare, my signaled sense of absence
must have added to everyone's silence
and that feeling of one leg less firmly planted.

Like the day I wore tennis shoes
from two different pairs to work, stared down
at unaligned logos; like the day I didn't zip my fly
and the Christian young man from the back row
made a sweet effort to whisper me into sensibility
by handing in papers that didn't need handing in
in order to get close enough to say so.
Think of reversals in dreams. The symbolism in lecturing
naked or arriving at the mall unbuttoned and undone.

At the public library, did the beribboned
volunteer think I meant *this* as my fashion
statement? Or did she consider me a variant
on the slowly moving unhoused who wait for the tall

glass doors to open each day? Or just didn't see me,
as me — someone who wears her clothes
generally the right way. Like the crepe-skinned woman
at the roadside antique store who was concerned
with the way the local paper had changed its format again.
Did I *agree*? Well, I did and I didn't.

In the truck, I buckled my seat belt to drive the last leg,
to drive to the gulf coast; buckled for the fifth time,
and suddenly saw my own seams.

This can be dealt with, I thought in shy woman panic.
Maybe apologies. Maybe a poem.

Where the mirage-filled road curves
toward the beaches, I hit my blinker, slowed onto sand
and watched the rear-views. I stripped for no one —
a quick OLE of cotton cloth while hot spring air pressed
seductively against the windshield. Then my T-shirt
settled around me, a safe second skin, a cloak
of renewed good citizenship
in the community of the rightly clothed.
Oh how simple to be eccentric
and how easy this day to be saved.
I straightened my shoulders, then, and drove
into a revealing, red-sunned April sunset.

FOOL FOR DOUBLES

I learn through symmetry, faces
I care for, paired features, but also
Sights seen: trees sentinel in place
At lakeside, as sky mimics water —

Or does water mimic sky? Think
About the balances of nature:
Hawk tears nestlings at sunset's brink,
Just one burrows down to safety.

Her paternal grandmother gave
My daughter endless social graces:
Transfusion of in-the-world faith,
A tongue-tip taste for gold jewelry.

Blood-twins tire of enforced collusion,
Faces like mirrors, same clothes' dull
Humor, their propinquitous prison,
Exchanging bit parts forever.

I learn through symmetry, faces
I care for: search for that wildness,
Uncommon conclusion, places
Never gone to, but moved toward.

I dream of a life dangerously twinned,
Of that *other*, who waits for words'
Slow journey, between hearts' thin-
Walled chambers of thought and desire.

THE ROCKING CHAIR, AGAIN

All furniture made, like all people
born, has its story, like this chair
bought in '73 when I was young
but thought I was older
and ripped off the fabric and lapped it in new
and liked it because it was old
(not because it was oak) with rounded
armrests and a high, comforting back.
I didn't feel ready to disturb
its uneven dark skin of syrupy lacquers
and let the cat sit too long
until the new cushions were coated in hair
and filled with tiny rips — he
worked his claws in an ecstasy there.

This spring, older, I felt young enough
to tackle the chair — to bring it to life.
March wind raged as I covered the kitchen floor
with an old cloth. I sanded. The cat
squeezed into a safe corner. The house
was covered by dry particles and dust,
cloth, tape measure and nails. The oak
came up fast, as if glad, white
and gray-white and ready for oil.
And I worked back, marveling I had not
done it before. Then I looked forward
to a future spent oiling the chair
and throwing off the cat and rocking
through a hundred seasons or more
when, gray-haired, slightly bald, bent,
I'd be on the floor, sanding again
and blessing a fate that let me care
for stories and craft and the serenity of work.

IN MEDIAS RES

Not in drought brown hills above the California coast.
Not in the 101 Drive in, Steve Miller on the stereo speakers.
Not in the foolish halls of high school.
Within hearing of the Pacific Ocean, Isla Vista, early morning,
                    surprising, not simple, quiet.
In a small two-person backpacking tent near the Austrian border.
During Ramadan, in Jerusalem, hostel in the Arab quarter,
                    tile bathrooms.
In between thinking and reading.
Within square boxes of student off-campus apartments.
After taking too much speed and jazz in Berkeley,
                    musical instruments on the walls.
Not in elegance, or in parents' houses, nubby bedspreads,
        clean guest towels, unused seashell soap.
Not on that bus, coast to coast, backpacks and midnight lake swims,
                    instead of showers.
Not in the Louvre.
Very precipitously in Cadaques.
Often only in imagination.
In a borrowed A-frame, cold, then wood heat warm,
                    during a Sierra storm.
Amid bat cries in a broken down barn.
On the banks of Cache Creek, long ago; now creek cut's gone.
Midnights at home, black cat purring, turning over and over.
While praising Southern Pacific, Palestrina, and being independent,
                    if poor.
On the river bank of the North Fork of the Eel River.
In the arms of a childhood friend.
As if reborn.
Rarely at noon.
Not carefully forewarned.
Not in Seattle or Pittsburgh.
In an office, Indian rug, custodian moving nearer down the corridor.

Not in the hammock, not on the ruins, plumed birds calling
                              across the pyramid's platform.
Under mosquito nets and ceiling fans, camel caravan threading
                              harmattan storms, artillery
          and a small war.
On the night cold grains of the Sahara, uranium trucks
                              cutting through darkness.
Not always with the ease of long familiarity.
Never in Greece.
On a couch near a door that could open,
                              waiting for something unknown.
Near rainwater in red rock, under a blossoming cottonwood,
                              pollen's blessing.
Before dawn.
Rarely all night long.
At high altitudes.
In the hurricane's eye of anger.
During circumlocutions of winter, mountains sculpting sky,
                              caribou crossing roadway,
          fast salmon spawn.
Not always with the ease of long familiarity.
Not carefully forewarned
Not in Saratoga or Toronto.
Often only in imagination.
To be reborn.
Stepping into the next story,
          just after the next story unfolds.

II. THE LIGHT AT THE END OF THE YEAR

NORTH FLORIDA NOCTURNE

Fall releases light
in slant golden sheets.
The yellow silk ignites
across this treetop and that treetop.
Still, there's an undertow of melancholy
in the Spanish moss.
Gray green. Bats furling. The earth turning inward.
All night, the constellations are rubbed clean.
At three a.m., again at six a.m., I look intently —
cold stones on the jeweler's velvet cloth.
Sometimes I consider these stars celestial dice
and I am working to make up the game.
I find messages from each year I've lived
weighing down corners of a rising Gulf breeze.
Salt scent. A headache. A hoot owl. A memory.
I dip into fertile blackness.
I'm seen. I become what I see.

ON PASSIONS

I'm ready to plant
three hundred day-lily roots —
warm afternoon dirt
heated like a body, furrowed
with my hands: I place each limb.

The lily roots — like
ginseng — seem human.
I name them — *Heartache,
Waiting, Distance, Impossible
Dream* — water them with my speech.

This strength in muscles
a long day's lesson. Such greenness:
sweat wraps like a caul
across my chest and drips salt-
sweet from collarbone to breasts.

Thirty days of water,
and roots will bloom this summer —
gold, red, apricot,
purple — accept nearly any
soil: propagate by division.

WITHOUT OCEANS

    for M.S.

I am astonished, at first, how anyone can
    have lived long yet not traveled to its lengths,
measured those rough antic swells, the rock cliffs and running
    tides, moon's messages: ebb, flood, neap. Madness,
really, to imagine growing old without oceans, overcome
    by dryness, hand held to eyes, eyeing the horizon,
like an Ishmael walking dryly inland to plant his oar. I imagine
    that the echoes of limitless waters haunt every ear
and then realize they must. I find ocean in canyon's frozen
    waves of red rock, see piscine shadows in alkali flats, sense
seas in some people's passing looks, matching my own peaceless
    need for walking out, out, across the rills of old tidelands
to a chilly edge, where, alone, the crash of crosscutting waters
    drowns the skee of seagull, slow bark of sea lions.
I don't mean brunch on the sand or the tossed beer bottle of the heart,
    but life-force, ocean you carry within, that rolls like leviathan,
sending upswelling waters to restore each wide dawn.

MY VISION, ONE SATURDAY IN MARCH

Geese wave
across the high blue soccer-field sky
while a chili red and an ardent purple team
use up their morning's portion
of testosterone.
In the grassy morning sunlight
legs windmill
shouts fountain from supple bodies.
hair dandelions in dervish patterns
and animal-nature rattles
out of full-bellowing lungs.
Some of these boys
will become executive dragons
uxorious manatee husbands
lions of commerce and control
heavy-headed mantises
at doctoral degree hoodings
sharp drinking deadbeat foxes
buckhorn sheep
who gavel out decisions
or coyotes in motorcycle leathers
men who leave
men who turn in time
into scratchy crickets
with comforting potbellies
with green memories
of sweet unfolding soccer strategies
like the perfect symmetry of the geese
they were too busy to see today
in flight.

GRAYTON BEACH

It's not only about the raccoon. We "named" her Roxy not Rocky because six slim nursing nipples showed when she raised on her hind-legs cupping delicate ratty paws for food, nearsighted, night sighted, attired in a black fur sleep masque, her fine-tuned nose finding rice cakes that my eager son threw like torpedoes anywhere but near, swaying while we talked to her, ignoring our entreaties to show us her children, not to get sick on granola bars, letting her animalify us as we personified her.

It's not only about the green algae, June grass, thick torn bits like underwater seed tufts, tinting Gulf tides turquoise then azure where the land drops off into low underwater foothills and undertow fingers our bodies. My children call waves overtows and fall like jellyfish onto quartz sugarsand, skitter sideways like sand crabs to bury themselves in the ooziest shallows. A seagull shrieks out his victory over a sandwich rind.

It's never about campgrounds. Smokers sit on the steps out front the showers, eyeing the Coke machine out of order, cuff their kids in the heat. Toddlers squeal into burrows of humid sleeping bags and teens saunter down to the lakeside, slapping insolently at biting flies. Green lizards learn the ways humans can entertain: a father ties blue tarp to trees, stokes a Coleman, pops a beer, a mother offers boxes and bags and scorched pot of food, entire extended families save their garbage in green, black, white plastic bags like hermit crabs festooning themselves, shudder at the real taste of sulphurwater, escape the stink of high-noon heat on too much tarpaulin and terrycloth.

There's something about lost beach towns, a three-way stop sign for the only three streets, rental agencies propping up empty duplexes. Established in 1890 on migrating dunes that sculpt dwarf magnolia. Slash pines leak turpentine, bonsai-ed myrtle oaks point wickedly upwards. The "downtown" restaurant opens and reopens and reopens, no French fries, just chips and sandwiches (and beer every night) and key lime pie, with real whipped cream that's not even listed on the menu, a place where we just have to talk to the counter guy who swaps REM for a Bach oratorio to ease his sunny morning hangover after a devoted Saturday night of work; he knows the clutter of dark hot air and drifting sighs across the patio, the drum of the beach, the howl of the ragged undistinguished animals from the hippie zoo down the road.

It's about learning names for the touristed and protected world. This one mile of beach between development communities forms an arroyo. Bees are hissing out of a sawn off branch whose joint cracked open to store their gold. It's about swales — low areas between high dunes. The topography of everything is worth naming, the biology of all worth savoring: yaupon, saw palmetto (my daughter stumbles gamely around each word), fetterbush, black rush, sweet bay, crookedwood, gallberry, and we exit the nature trail onto the bomb-blast-white beach, blink away shade and fungi, erosion and salt marsh, wood-boring insects give way to salt spray and wind pruning and the park ranger has tagged another sea turtle nest, stakes and orange tape marking out her mysterious four foot square. We see her giant flipper trail heave up from the tide line in undulating circles followed by the sharp incising of a foolishly small tail. Gentle dents that must cover eggs and the grunting slide back down, in the dark, to amniotically warm water.

It's how, late on the second day, I see my son and daughter playing. One is buried to the neck in sand, a grinning pumpkinhead of sea blasted pleasure. One makes motions: flippers out a path, kisses the dunes, edges toward sea oats, sea-turtle inspired, baptized.

GARDENIA

Eleven white petals the shape of flattened baseball bats,
        white-turning-brown edges curled back.

Sexual parts looking like an upside-down spider —
        five tawny stamen legs waving toward this
        lonely, light-yellow banana-shaped pistil.
Meaty green leaves in lilypad layerings but not in lilypad sizes.
Formed like citrus leaves but a deeper, glossy green.

A white, yeast-infection-thick-scent, like heaven gone bad.
A bottle of fume blanc.
A musty secret, something kept moist for ages,
        edges blurring back toward raw earth.
A sky on the Fourth of July: heavy humidity expected, in fact, invited.
The secret of all indulgence, overkill, and destruction
        and the draw of the same.

Like a funeral *and* a birth: this is an occasion. A moment waited-for
        that arrives, too large, too big, too fast.
Like fantasies.
Like expensive and undercooked meats.
Like guilt, glut, sin, but squat —
        not roses on their imperious high-heeled stalks
        not snapdragons, frivolous and blown in the winds.

When a girl first feels her hips touch her palms at night without asking.
When a girl first pushes cotton sheets out of the bottom
                      of the tightly tucked bed.
When a girl first eats her own tears and likes them: too sweet,
        too light to lunch on for long yet
        irresistible.
When a girl first passes her message from hand to hand.

The gardenia is re-invented.

REPORT

Two feet above the belly-feather blue-green gulf waters,
twenty yards below my wide-open, wind-filled windows,
in a line, two-thousand wing-spread winter ducks flew,
formed a ribbon of flight, mobius-strip of follow the leader,

twenty yards below my wide-open, wind-filled windows
while I watched. I thought *no one will believe this.*
Formed a ribbon of flight, mobius-strip of follow the leader,
while I watched. I thought I *can never describe this.*

While I watched, I thought *no one will believe this,*
as I pressed myself against a hand of astonishing sky.
While I watched, I thought I *can never describe this,*
learned then that to see, not to say, was the day's bright lesson.

While I watched I thought *no one will believe this,*
two feet above the belly-feather blue-green gulf waters,
learned then that to see, not to say, was the day's bright lesson:
in a line, two-thousand wing-spread winter ducks flew.

PRESCRIPTION FOR WINTER

It is good to bake, to look ahead,
To freeze fresh food for long winters,
And good to sing in the morning,
Cleaning the house from neck to toes
Before the cold rains. It is good
To pack and unpack summer things
And winter things, to show yard plants
To the indoor shelf. Still, time is so
Precious. The small song at the back
Of your neck, the swift flight of your hands,
The muffled twist of your body at night
Tell you: don't wait for showers of birds,
For the growth of trees, for love
Stern and solid in the pit of your back.
Take nothing to a place you have barely
Dreamed of. Walk faster and faster,
And the earth will pass like a sweet
Untamed vision beneath your hard feet.

HOW TO BE A SHELL

Be quiet. Wink. Let tides
turn you upside down. Quick,
sink, when a child hurls you
into foam. Keep your
mouth shut or speak out
of one side of your mouth
with your single velvet lip.

TERZANELLE ON DROUGHT

Drought is the state we are in here.
Blue bowl of sky. No clouds. No rain.
Days steal moisture, parch our tears.

We would speak, if speech could explain.
Slow dust devils; summer fruit unswelled.
Blue bowl of sky. No clouds. No rain.

Or speak to break silence and meld
Together, dance down rains, shape prayer
Against dust devils. Summer fruit won't swell.

Sun hangs high in thin cloudless air.
We share cool sheets, cotton on skin,
Braid limbs to a dance the shape of prayer,

Praise what insists on going missing.
Our bodies mysterious as oceans,
We share cool sheets of cotton on skin

Until summer falters and ends.
Drought is the state we are in here.
These bodies mysterious as oceans.
Day steals moisture, returns it as tears.

IF OVER YOUR SHOULDER
THE HANGNAIL MOON

If over your shoulder the hangnail moon
Had never shown, the sky not cast its glowing
Reds up to the stars, or stars not ballooned
Into fantastic shapes, we'd still have known
To walk behind the house in evening's heat
And talk about the day and simple pleasures,
To touch in simple ways, to find time sweet
As we scuffed the warm dust at our leisure,
For summer nights are meant to fold away
For winter when ice takes us in our bones
And empties out our images of sky
To white and gray and locks us in our homes,
Then flings the sun much farther from our sight
And turns the moon cold in its bath of night.

TO GET RAIN

If it would only rain, I'd be shameless.
I'd allow this yellow, two-gallon container of chlorine to eat away
    the plastic liner of my swimming pool. I'd promise never
    to fill a hole of dust with captive blue water again.
I'd picket the manufacturers of small upstart gods — little green
    sprinklers with names like waterworks or whirlingwaters
    or rainmaker.
I'd make sure every dog in the neighborhood jumped awake
    at 4:30 a.m. to howl its applause at the round July moon, to
    chase the newspaper-delivery stationwagon into the last
    cul-de-sac before thunder breaks.
I'd concede that wind chimes hung on the lower palm bracts don't
    sound as good without those round seductive beads of
    moisture to amplify their windy symphonies.
I'd listen all night to the Morse code of clouds as it plays
    across the skylights. I'd play my secrets back
    and I'd never feel cheated.
I'd add my few tears to the red earth, stir them in. The dust devil
    this raises would rip my best shirt from the clothesline,
    send it flying across sagebrush, pampas grass, pine forest,
    sea oats, St. Augustine lawns, begging: please, today, please,
    today — please.
Why, if it would only rain, I'd be shameless.
Again.

ANOTHER CELESTIAL CIRCUIT IN NORTH FLORIDA

I walk out into a dog morning, before leaping flames
of clouds are unleashed, swipe the shooting star down
        with my free hand,
    hear the owls educate fools with long *hoos*,
    taste humid dew a mile-thick on my forearms,
    smell the froggish night steal away
    look at the tight hat of constellations
    and say a secret name, twice.
I was meant to be another Robert, born in Duluth.
I was never meant to be a fool, hooting morning-long at sleeping owls.
It's night that worries me most: it climbs up my back over low hills
    fitch-like and stealthy.
If I said a fitch was a polecat, weasel, it would be so
    for the time it takes to say
    "But I promised not to be gone anymore weekends."
Those blue weekends of desire.
Who expects to take a cold morning shower?
Like thinking Orion would step down out of the heaven,
    unbuckle his belt.
Like calling her Ariadne, and asking for help getting out
        sooner, soonest.
I would expect, the heat of southern mornings
    could shake up the armadillo in you
    and make you wonder where it is you're going.
Going home, going to a hotel, going all weekend, going to hell,
    the gods and goddesses rearrange themselves in the quilted sky.
"Sleep" is the message. Or was it just "shoot the dog"?
Die sensualische Sprache, has always challenged me.
The dog howls at the humid trees and the trees howl back
    Spanish Moss has girl-fights with humid leaves.
If the fitch can survive this night, why so can we.

BACK CORNERS

Azaleas lost under spidery vines,
vines that thrust blue cups into light
beneath a bent live-oak, bowed by near
hurricanes and winds that arrive
mostly when I sleep.
                I sleep by windows
screened toward hands of gardenia —
scent of white flowers and flesh —
slick green leaves curled inward
like dreams.
                Like dreams, piles
of hedge and grass, dried clipped flower heads,
heat up against the fence, blackened, tawny
burn apart over time.
                This time, I lean
the wheelbarrow near monkey grass,
African iris, tomato wire in empty cones,
pieces of broken, earth-red potsherds,
volunteer marigolds that grow sideways.
                To one side
and down slope, at the spot worn free
of Augustine, oak and azalea tendons
wrestle over and under, dive into muddy
earth.
                Earth breeds
endless rills of unexpected wildness —
I find tangled, hard breathing growth,
ripe clatter of mockingbird, cardinal, woodpecker —
below jet trail of heron.
                Heron, and now cranes
from the north, stitch these small acres together
into a southern back corner crazy-quilt.

THE FARM

Walking the fields that were great-grandfather's farm,
        stubble holds me back. Root claws reach up and hang on
a shoe strap. Dirt heaps around stalk tomb stones; a fallen
army of plants rests here. The farm comes with death. The
fall ground untilled and unturned is leeched gray from rain
and woven with weeds. At the borders of fields, trees strip
themselves of leaves. Wind points them to cow paths, to collapsed outbuildings, to an endless sky, rampant with gray. Up
slope at the homestead, I walk through the doorway, lintels
as nonexistent as the floor. I walk to unframed windows.
Without walls, the view is as big as the house was small,
twenty by twenty sod feet, earth borrowed whole. Now, the
sod dissolved, supports fall down into stacks of logs. Windows, if they ever came, were carted off to mirror other descendants, other scavengers' faces. Nothing to say Ole Berg
ever left Norway, landing here to farm all his days, nothing to
name grandmother, a child in a headscarf, who remembered
the dark farm mornings, who chased a shrill hen free from
her nest, eggs glowing like dreams, nothing but me, setting
up house in their place.

TO SEED

The wider beds unkempt, red clay pots
                broken, kicked butt-up
so their mix of coffee-ground soil and white foam pellets
splays rain-washed fans across
                fist-sized magnolia seeds,

and these magnolia leaves burnished like the etched copper bowl
found and lost,
lost and found
in a box that travels from shelf to shelf
across the years.

Rose bushes
                a sprawl of thorny legs,
              an unremarked driveway can-can,
but they'll outlast any occupation, by damn.

                Gone wild, tough camellia stems
brace against old shears
as I clip this dusk,
unwind sycophantic vines,
sweep roughed terrazzo porch
burnish its cosmetic faults
into yard's dark.

                Fallow. Gone a little wild. To seed.

Try not to pare too much, too fast,
take time to feel out borders,
contours, the way light strikes
pecan and pine, links lawn to shrub to fence.

Think of others, trimming back, closing up,
for the summer, the season,
abandoning everything that once was
for the duration.

THURSDAY'S WEATHER

> *Mostly sunny, no rain, low 43, high 67.*
> — Tallahassee Democrat

> *It's like anything, you can't see the possibilities until they engulf you.*
> — E-mail from Kate

In December, kudzu vines tangle into skeins of brown hair,
dogwood fans out, golden bright gasp of fall,
and red Chinese maples shoot up like hands, as I drive past.

On these roads, two-laned, arched over with trees
congested and too-often traveled, my thoughts run and drift
again and again, a slow wake-up of speed bumps,

music enters the airstream and words seep out —
my son asking two nights ago why all songs are about love,
asking what digital time it is, asking what each billboard says.

It's a season mostly of windows, trunk of live oak as lush
in its rained upon greenness as my daughter's changing body;
she who wakes each morning filled with new liquids and secrets,

says she loves me more than anyone and some she hates me
more than anyone — braids around me like summer vines
and bends me to her, pins down my free branches voluntarily.

Newly laid gray sod waits next summer's rains and aching heat.
Morning's horizon pinks the clouds, teases them into bleedings,
crimson striations. My meditation is our lesson, re-learned each day:

there are only so many ways to greet a destination — with words
in silence, careful observation. Each entrance has its hesitation: I see
a room full of people and then I see you. I see a familiar road

and then I've driven on, into another country, a certain
but unfamiliar one. Inside, our transformation,
while along the way, regular weather, typical trees.

OF SUMMER

— Fairbanks, Alaska

Our sun chases the horizon all night.
Day turns upside down, and evening
bleeds into dusk, that is — dawn —
unfolding wild rose and blue bells
like pointillist dabs on quaking aspen
canvas, backdrop to a dandelion-strewn lawn.

Only the Arctic loves the dandelion.
Sun after sun after sun after sun,
the yellow lions of summer number winter hours
that were lost to darkness
when dry quilts of snow mulched spring.

Spring comes late, comes even while we strain
looking for it. Leaves unfurl with time-lapse quickness
and one morning,
at three a.m.,
in gaining light,
the dandelions
roar out their mouthful of gold.

APPROACHING ENNUI

Spring's rude sap slows me. I think
of sleeping within a moon-cauled hammock.
Of a friend running away from his family
to hang himself by the heartstrings of hope. Of a toad
beneath the back door water faucet, expectant
and bloated. Filled with undrained, sun-scalded water,
lawn hoses drag me into unexpected tug-of-wars.
I've found it's impossible to approximate a lightning storm
so invent my own weather.
                    Sky clouds over with thoughts.
Gardenias compound packets of gardenia perfume.
A mourning dove freezes when I walk past rustling
newsprint, teasing her with: I *see you sweetheart*.
She flies madly into a thorny ground-palm. A*s if I care*,
I whisper, looking for the yard cat.
Drifts of lovebugs pair in tuxedo black, dragging
each other to easy, stupid deaths.
                    I pound at the air
around them; wipe moth-green pollen from every
ledge; test a window pane for its guillotine-balance.
I could almost argue for stopping right here,
right now, before the city drains itself around a southern
summer, slipping away by coastal car or business jet.

Sick-call of suchness today. The old dog dreams me into
that leg-jerk feel of *what, again*? I make plans, the same ones,
to hold out long enough, to cut a deal with dawn.

ON GIVING AND FINDING GIFTS

> *Paul Valery speaks of the 'une ligne donné' of a poem. One line is given to the poet by God or by nature, the rest he has to discover for himself.*
> — Stephen Spender

It's summer. We are all writing about walking —
walking up Irish headlands with unexpected lovers,
walking around a Florida lake, talking

our way into metaphors. Expectancy hovers
over each waking moment, walking next door
to play with an imagined child and maneuvering

that meeting into words. Walking is a poor
substitute for the past but a good way to find it.
Walking to the southwest, knocking door to door

at vacant addresses. Same summer, I visit
with a friend; insomniac, she's memorizing Emily
Dickinson and starting conversations with this

or that irrefutable line, walking into the sea
of Emily's gifts. All our lines must be gifts.
If we find them in our brains' deep pockets, free

and unencumbered, of course we make them fit.

CALL ME ISHMAEL

> *It is no less difficult to write a sentence in a recipe than sentences in* Moby Dick. *So you might as well write* Moby Dick.
> — Annie Dillard

I am busy writing *Moby Dick*.
I've been to the beach
and measured the sands.
I've made a list of what is in
and what is out when writing
or when cooking. I think
about menus enough
to qualify as whale-obsessive.
So I might as well concoct this story.

I mean here I am in Tallahassee,
trying to grow basil for summer pesto
and now I have to wreathe my whale
in basil garlands. Diving, it will make a sound,
reminiscent of choiring frogs on Lake Jackson
whose summer need moves leviathan-like
over this sleepy town.

I've collected sea grasses.
I've thought and I've listened,
arranged Gulf coast seashells
into a checker game.
Each time I make a move,
I start a new chapter.

Hungry, I reheat
clam chowder, whale steaks
my daughter's tuna fish
and resolutely, an author at last,
I start to begin to finish
my big white book.

FROM A BOTTLE

Alligator Point, Florida

Consider the beautiful black thoughts of an anhinga bird
wandering, from estuary onto this wide gray belly of gulf water.
Or the blue heron, elegant as chop sticks.
She broods with awful fastidiousness
while seaweed-filled waves
knit anklets out of cross-currents.
Warm air holds down this thought,
warmer water buoys up beneath it.
At shoreline, this small glass raft nudges coquina. They dig
into sand with a bubbling gasp of group thought — *Get away*
or *Come away?* — the message hardly matters.

Water edges in like a hermit crab,
soaks ink from the wafers of paper I've written on.
In ceremonious collusion, I experience
that Davey Jones' locker feeling — cast ideas forward
just before napping, captive, through the late afternoon.
Then, summer dusk and a bedspread of darkness
drops down like a seiner's net. Anhinga and heron
lift beakily, cumbersomely, into their last-second escape.
Tomorrow, dawn will pour into the narrow neck
and these sentences will whisper out
with a water bird's comfortable hunger.

MY ARMADILLO

— buries omnivorous nose
in Augustine grass spikes
(heated all day in fall brightness,
they store a musty sweetness in their roots).

— takes things as he finds them,
shows unguarded belly to almost no one
unless the new moon calls him
with milky changing lips.

— unfolds his armor slowly, plate
by shiny plate, until he senses
danger in mulch-pile or hedge-dark,
(back-corner places that I cannot see).

— curls into a bone-white crescent
at the sound of lizards in dry oak leaves,
at the wind of footsteps, at the touch of voices
from my open windowsills.

My armadillo,
gone each morning,
leaves his restless notice
in newly uprooted patches —
— in this dawn's wet greengrass.

COASTAL

Lost in a Florida tundra
of sandspurs, weeds, grasses,
her old mower roars and shouts at the gulls
who spy her out: small figure on a large shore.

Squat sago palms, Spanish
bayonets, sharpened on summer,
pierce flesh like butter. Calves stinging,
she pushes against potato vines, tenacious
and abundant. Afternoon limps to a sweaty finish.

Breeze gathering across thunderheads
scatters birdseed from feeders
as certainly as the cardinals and doves.
Upended on palm trunk, woodpecker
harvests a grim tithe of palmetto bugs.

Beyond a sea oat palisade
of golden, inedible grain, the yard
plunges into dunes. Blue heron tacks past,
furled into a compact galleon,
horizontal plumb-line creating scale, horizon.

Sandpipers, she's concluded, snip furtive bites
from her thoughts, thieve them into gulf foam;
otherwise, why run so far, so fast?
Mosquitoes drink as if at a fountain.

Razor angled with slick accuracy,
she showers, slices open bloody volcanoes
that track ankles like new archipelagos.
The coastal day races shorewards again
and blood swirls with salt into the shower drain.

WISHING SPRING: A GHAZAL

The cardinal shakes his cape of red blades in the morning light,
eclipses his mate, who falls from the roof-ridge halo of light

to the darkness of the cat's claws. Dull brown stays dull in porch light.
The squirrel on the fallen oak, freezes, stunned by morning-glory light.

My son says — I had a dream, the sun passed the moon,
                                                      blocked out light.
Daybreak fills with cardinal's whistle: worship and call. Light

won't warm spring eggs. It takes a mate. He needs to pull
                                               another into his light.
Tulips, despite the morning frost, unfurl meaty green leaves
                                                   into thin light.

My daughter unfurls each morning, reluctantly, blinking at the lights
I turn on. I try to call her out of sleep, body growing lighter

with growing, lost in eclipses of sleep. Slow to greet the light
and then slow to let it go. The cat responds to longer light.

Her tawny fur clumps, ready to fly like dandelion seed into light
spring air. The cardinal wife escapes into the light

beyond all light, where sudden dead and newly born come to light.
What does "eclipse" mean? and *What does "Bishop" mean?*
                                                 my son says, alight

with the day's questions. It's a church office, I say. I bless this light.
Bless light rising and setting. Bless squirrels, cardinals, cats,
                                                     children — light.

THE SUMMER SEASON

In this season
dark animals cross the roads
under a crop-duster's moon.

In this house, handed an empty
skull and told its story, I listen
to rock and roll. The tight
tan molars and the yearning
tusks weight down my hand
with the merciless heft of bone
as the guts of the music
help to wrap me in night dreams:
    carnivores outside make paths
      through fields and mountain ranges,
      keen eyes bleached by starlight.

The music of the hunt
is so familiar. It comes singing
across acres of tomatoes and beets.
It comes singing across the scree
and rubble of the cradling Sierras.
It comes singing into this
small house in a hot river city,
singing in the empty eyes
of this tiny and powerful skull.

Many are in the room but few listen.
I place the smooth teeth close
to my ear — animal conch, oracle.
We are lost in the roar of records
and unnoticed in a summer room
as it sings to me and I sing back,
jaws moving with an instinctive
and a loving motion.

THE LIGHT AT THE END OF THE YEAR

Goes with us into sleep.
A withered crone's ivory kiss,
Sears our foreheads
With a luminous darkness.
Her skirts drag over the landscape.
Yellowed summer fans
Are falling like paddles
From the trees. Birds
String berry necklaces
And fill their down purses,
Then spout upward
Into streams of cold air.

In summer,
Her lap was a grain field growing in heat.
Her arms a lake's edge,
   Where boats drift and nudge docks
   In the dusk.
Only her hair,
Ice gray, like the distant peaks,
Held the secrets of change
   And death.

When the sun recedes,
   When the fall shakes out and inspects
   Its salvage of tissue paper,
   Skeletons of insects and leaves,
   Its light beams quilted
   Into patterns of orange and green,
   When the long afterglow
   That we beg with our eyes fades,
She is the one who pulls down the shades
And gathers up in great folds our dreams.

GULF SHELLS

form sand dunes
when their hearts break,
hold firm lips together
in muscular kisses
until one midnight
moonlight seduces them
and the lodgers slip out —

Gulf shells wink at children
in sunlight; frustrate
the fussy gulls;
hold hors d'oeuvres,
memories, grit, or pearls;
outline shower
curtains and towels
in chic catalogues.

Gulf shells define a beach
I'm on my way to —
they cut and cleave,
clutter shoreline as they please,
exhibit the lines water wears —
salty markers of
my wet and windy age.

WHERE THE HUMMINGBIRD SIPS, THERE SIP I: AN APPRECIATION

> *I send you withal a little Box, with a Curiosity in it ... the curiously contrived Nest of a Humming Bird, so called from the humming noise it maketh whilst it flies. 'Tis an exceeding little Bird, and only seen in Summer, and mostly in Gardens, flying from flower to flower, sucking Honey out of the flowers as a Bee doth; as it flieth not lighting on the flower, but hovering over it, sucking with its long bill a sweet substance.*
> — The Honorable John Winthrop,
>   Governor of Connecticut, 1670.

She dances messages
beyond my writing-desk window-pane,
raises questions,
yanks them away again.
Flying forwards, backwards,
picaflor, beija flor,
huitzitzil, chuparosa.
Blossom-picker, flower-kisser,
rays-of-the-sun, rose-sucker.
Weighs as little as a penny,
or not much more. She's
Buff-bellied, Lucifer, Roufous, Ruby,
Violet-crowned, Broad-tailed, and Calliope.

She's what I want to be.

She navigates my stanzas.
She takes my words away
to throaty scarlet penstemon;
to meaty trumpet flowers,
calls on hibiscus, sinks
into summer's columbine,
pollinates a cactus blossom.

She's catch as catch can.

Truth is —
she's a whore for red,
scavenger of nectar, syrup, honey,
maintains the metabolic rate
of thought. Her wings long hands
in service of her tongue —
even as she begins,
she's at top speed,
rising phoenix-like
from another flower-flame.

I invite her
to inhabit me.

She takes after my own heart.
She's my cross-dressing
dandy of a girl —
too busy to make-up
too busy to stay,
frivolous ruby for her gorget,
head crowned in tourmaline.
White and brown belly-feathers
beneath that finery.

She's dashing,
in her hurry-up way.

She is at risk —
compounded into amulets
and hummingbird soap,

powdered, or stuffed —
turned by bounty hunters
into a potent corpse
to "dominate, conquer
and attract" *amor* —
sold with a preprinted prayer
and a red silken bag.
A sacrificed bride's finery,
an Aztec warrior's
shimmering cloak.

She's insight. She's action.

She's fragile but not frail.
She failed geology —
for her bones of sparkling dust
cannot be fossilized,
cannot be saved.
She is kachina Tocha,
the Humming Bird.
When the Gods required speed
and good looks, they called
on their feather dart.

I claim her as kin.

She's past the window,
she's past the garden fence,
a Curiosity with curiosity,
Just out of hearing,
just out of sight —
stars and constellations
spark into fires.

CENTERS OF GRAVITY

— Fairbanks, Alaska

We throw out our laughter
Against incoming air.
The confetti flecked
Mixing bowl of summer
Caps down upon the city
And for three slim months
We tread sun like water.
Day dreams and night dreams
Meet in two hours each midnight.

The first morning I rolled over
Into love's arms
I knew I should have known:
Gravity and all logic end there.
Years of staring at chest hair
I learned to dissolve skin
And search through interiors —
Charms in the ribcage:
Amulets of terror, cowry shells
Laced to hand-dyed red leather;
Hoarded sovereigns
Stamped on a shuddering die press
And tarnishing in the heart's dissolve.

Corpuscles? I saw centers
Within centers. Ace iridologist,
I saw rings in the sleeping eye.
Layers and circles imposed
On raw molars. I was a tree surgeon
Of teeth, for tools a cool tongue.
I could augur good or ill

From callus and a constellation of moles
Or call down blessings on that ruffle
Of child's hair that threatened
My young man's beardless face.

This summer, this sun will be
A rude tipping against seasons
And a rare entry into the unlaced
Corset of my self. You stay through
All divinings, yes, no, yes, no,
Until the leavening of life
Finds us pitched full against each day.

Come winter, a single tone
Will shatter all colors, flash
Of geese into a glacial sky
And our laughter will freeze upright,
A wave to the dancing lights
That go with us into such darkness.

III. THE NEW WORLD

JOURNEY

    after Peter Fruchin's *Book of the Eskimo*

Like a Dane who has spent
Many years in the Arctic,
I return to you
Through days of ice
And winter darkness.
After eating the meat,
The hides, extra clothing,
And digging the dogs out
To devour them too,
I stayed alive.
Losing some toes,
Going blind in white sun,
Fasting as game
Moved beyond reach,
Setting the traps
Then finding them empty,
Waiting by blowholes
But scaring the seals,
I return to the settlement
With stories for you.
Like a Dane sitting quietly,
Amazed by the banquet
And warmed by the lights,
Who forgets as he eats
And praises the hard life
He once cursed,
I have brought myself
As a message from darkness
To you.

THE NEW WORLD

The far horizon was a flat line where
The sky and ocean met like thin sealed lips,
And cold waves slapping on the ship would steer
Us firmly toward the west. Suns slipped
Into the night and still no land appeared.
We cursed the impulse that produced the trip
That travel to a new place could create
Such panicked pleasure and this sense of fate.

But when the coastal birds arrived to perch
In rigging overhead, we tried to forget
The storms and ghostly sirens that emerged
In dreams, tempting us to cast adrift
All caution and all foresight in the search
For change, adventure and forgetfulness.
As youth prefers love's endless ferment,
Adventurers search for unknown continents.

And distant miles still at sea, we sensed
The new world, its prehistoric coast
Upthrust to clouds, and forests, dense
And fragrant, that fell to foothills and closed
Upon the salt-white beaches in a redolence
Of scent: crushed peppers mixed with jungle growth.
Smells interlocked with shore winds and floated
A promise of land's substance to our boat.

We'd pace a restless length of deck and speak
Of that faint ephemeral fragrance:
Like a sunrise swiftly lost to the breaking
Of a ruder morning and the slow events
Of shipboard routine, like the sleek
Arc of dolphins alternately rending

The wet gray blanket of the moving ocean
Where we watched them rise and disappear again,

Or like the sad, continuous receding
Of what we left behind, the scent reminded
Us of night and the final meeting
With those we loved, or, leaving, tried to entwine
In love. It made us long for land, for heat
And growth and seasons passing in their time.
Just when nostalgia filled us like narcotic,
We recalled the reasons why we left.

Then petrels bore the smell down from the sky
As if to test us; land and safety were
Still days away. We watched them swerve and fly
Across our fluted sails. We'd come too far
For second thoughts, for plans to go awry,
And cheered the fresh wind and the northern star.
Our passage soon would be complete and then
We'd start our venture on that fragrant land.

HILLS

1 **Five Trees**

Behind the city's water tanks
First cut by sheep and cattle tracks,

A trail led up the angled slopes
Of hills, slipped in summer's envelope

Of grass, wind-plaited, tinder brown.
Beside a stand of trees, I looked down

To watch the city move below.
Hardened to inspection, a crow

Held its aimless float, then flapped away,
And left the breezes of midday.

The trees were moving in a dance
Along the twisted wire fence.

And then I heard the first car horn
That rose above the insect hum.

It tripped my sudden downhill race
At an erratic childhood gait.

2 California Wildfire

The shoulders of the hills
Were blacker for the crown.
Flame ate the sky away
In up leaping arcs.
The base stretched from earth
To the stones of stars
And curled from ocean front
To the brow of mountains.
No castle, a *home* was only a hope
And *wind*, a barbaric word
On tired lips.

DAWN SONG

Capay Valley, California

Aubaude, I read, any lyric
Suggesting morning,
So I write to you:

"It was hard to leave
so early and in the dark.
I lifted the covers and rose
Into the coatish weight
Of predawn: moist in nostril,
Heavy in bone, chains
On the dogs clinking
And raw snorts
As they waited outdoors
Eager to bay at the new sun.

"I waited too, propped up in bed,
Halfway in, halfway out,
Toes in the nether world,
Frosted still by sleep,
One hand benedicting your hair.
I heard the bats nesting
In gunny sacks, flat
And rotten, that hung
Along the ridgepole of the barn.
They chittered and flapped.
Darkness eased by a hue.

"It was hard to imagine
Bats nesting,
Folding and stroking
Their leaf-rough skin.

Passion: straw bones,
The clutch of attenuate hands.
'The only mammals
With the power of true flight.'
Giving up mammal heaviness
For a stringy dance,
A sonar loop-the-loop.

"When I started the car
And turned into the road,
Low beams on,
Bats flattened in the headlights,
Arrowheads without shafts.
I saw the skin cased fingers,
The free sweeping claws
Raised as if to say,
'Someday, you too.'
I saw them disintegrate,
Caught between the lamps
And the first flashes of morning.
They seemed to carry my heart
With them, into the day's shadows,
As I took the next curve."

THE ICE PALACE

Ships one-hundred-twenty blocks
each week to the cold
vaults. Caterers commission feathered
swans for cruise ships. Old
rags warm the hands
of plant workers. Crushed

ice, shattered, newly crushed,
means effort lost: thirty-seven-gallon blocks
fashioned here for forty-seven years by hand
require two days each in a cold
saltwater bath. *The Palace* sheds are old
patched wood, and workers shiver there, a feather

chill down the neck; if feather
feeling spreads, all senses are crushed.
It's deadly to stay thirty minutes in old
forming rooms where blocks
grow shoulder to white cold
shoulder, never touched by hand.

Yet it takes firm hands
to spray crushed ice, feather-
light, across truckloads of corn, keep cold
the fast-picked crops, before heat crushes
a farmer's hopes. Down the block
at *Sam's Spot* they tell old

disaster stories, tally loans: surely old
hopes melt slowly. *The Palace* boss hands
out checks to Mike and Keith for blocks
of perfection, little white-feather-
ice, few impurities, no chips, no crushed.
edges. Ice sculptors pay well for these cold

crystals of light. Safe from cold
wind of foreclosure, the shed's always been old
like the leached and hail-crushed
fields of crops. But just come round, hands
out, plastic bag billowing and feathering
between, for your fill of broken or blocked.

The Ice Palace stocks clear deep blocks, sells cold
for drinks, or carved swans, feathers sharp as hopes, craft old
as dirt farmers' hands: earnest, nicked, and crushed.

GARDEN

> *O peoples and nations of every language,*
> *you are commanded, when you hear the sound*
> *of horn, pipe, zither, triangle, dulcimer,*
> *music and singing of every kind, to prostrate*
> *yourselves, and worship the golden image*
> *which King Nebuchadnezzar has set up.*
> Daniel 3: 4-5

On the empty plain
where Nebuchadnezzar
spent his dreams, I stand

and imagine that the distant hills
made his captive queen sad.

I appreciate a man
who builds his bride a garden
four hundred feet high,
who builds an ark of vegetation
and consumes a city of workers.
I understand
if a woman walks the walls,
a man must tend the well
so she may drink.

The sky is burning, dreams
come at dawn in the torrid lands:
a giant figure with
head of gold and breast
of pure silver,
belly and thighs of bronze,
legs of iron, feet of iron

and clay. The clay
dissolves, the body
falls, the mind awakes.

It is day. The king rises
and would call a counselor.

How his hair grows
like a goat's and his nails
like eagles' talons.

He becomes an ox grazing,
drenched by the dews of heaven
in his madness.

I walk along the empty
grounds and place
all things where they
used to be: palace, city,
the royal gardens,
Babylon's king, lost like a beast
in the desert, diviners marveling
over a dismembered statue,
or a dream,

the queen, parched
and homesick for the shade
of mountains, a shade herself
walking the sands in moonlight.

But no gardens
stand out against the sky.

All that remains
this dawn: the cellar
and a dry well

where slaves and animals
toiled endlessly in darkness.

THE BRICKMAKER'S SINKHOLE AT GORON DUTSE, NIGERIA

When you dive the first time
after a long work day, dust
is scraped off by the flat blades
of lily pads. As you break through,
water flies up your descending skin
like all the winds of the world
but without their howl.
Who cares how far down you go,
free, eyes closed?

The water was brown in the sinkhole
from debris and the brickmakers' art.
Dried bricks took the occasional print
of lily stalk, broken pot,
sharp goat hoof. Everything
discarded by the neighborhood,
crumbled and rolled to the water's edge.
Boys played there
and splashed toward the big rock.
They jumped and jumped all day,
eyes closed.

One morning the pool was lined
with boys and men in white
feast-day robes, diving
and diving, play ritualized,
eyes open.

The dead swimmer dragged out
was wrapped in his father's cloak,
in his father's arms, and the procession
of neighbors formed.

How far a young man can fall
at the end of the day
tired and trembling
on the hard edge of rock,
eyes closed.

The crowd parted
around the slowly moving father
like the lily flowers around
the diver who goes down.

BLUE MOON I: AN ELEGY

I rustle Sunday papers
into a bouquet
of uncertain information
and study Mario Zacchini.

Last of five human cannonball
brothers who died yesterday
just short of a safe landing
into this night's blue moon sky.

Of the seven brothers, five
chose to sail at 90 miles an hour
above their slack-jawed peers,
over the fake rainbow of the Ferris wheel.

How the other two, earthbound
would have flinched when the screen door
slammed back, when that day's
triumphant cannonball brother

dropped his clumsy padded helmet
to grab a beer,
to brag,
to roar at the sky.

How they
must have drifted
like asteroids breaking free
of biological gravity

walked stoic or stubborn,
from the family house

to the family yard,
inspecting newly emptied heavens.

One stands lost in meditations
under a storm-blown palm tree.
The other, the youngest,
turning down the family trade,

feels his girlfriend's hands,
orbits anyway on a slow-rocking
summer porch
as the evening ebbs away.

The eldest, Mario,
is possibly somewhat drunk
on wind and velocity,
a bit tired of compression

and eye-searing speed
and somewhat lonely too
having arrived so quickly,
and again safely.

Each brother feels
another blue moon rise.
A horizon where Sputnik blinked
brightly, like the family fortune.

The carnivals gone, carnies
retired into Florida sunlight,
A daredevil's adrenaline ebbs
into the indigo of space.

Think of all the places
the bluest moon can't illuminate.
All the places we —
cart wheeling, cannonballing,

curiously conflicted and eager —
we so human, with or without
our gravid blue lamp,
dare not, can not, quite see.

LOVERS AND TRIBES

> We die containing a richness of lovers and tribes, tastes we have swallowed, bodies we have plunged into and swum up as if rivers of wisdom, characters we have climbed into as if trees, fears we have hidden in as if caves. ... We are communal histories, communal books. We are not owned or monogamous in our taste or experience.
> — Michael Ondaatje, *The English Patient*

That summer, friends gathered, and we plunged
Into our tourist natures, traveled beyond thunder

And monsoon threat, left mountains for mesas, mapped
Canyons and stark cliff dwellings, in a manner half

Humorous as our black over-full Volkswagen
Ferried our clan: Spare shirts, thermoses, gear-laden

And talkative, from de Chelly to Verde to Chaco Canyon
Where we quieted before that stone book of emptiness. Then

Unpacked, two by two, from the car to swallow
Its ages under afternoon heat. Single-file followed

The dry river of our selves, lost interest
In anything but sheer rock face, how it just missed

Collapsing, frozen in geology's massive
Free-fall, to scoured sand. At the narrow passage

Into the kiva, I saw your figure go before me, disappear
Like my breath around a turn. Say, two-thousand years

Since community hopes brushed those dun walls,
As the lands emptied, life draining, falling away

From Chaco's honey-combed center. Spirits faded.
Car doors slammed. We drove west, through deserted space,

The long unpaved road back, and our remaining days.

DIARY, PHOTOGRAPHER, 1850: THE YUCATAN

after F. Catherwood and J.L. Stephens

Three days out. A tremendous storm. I could barely make the upper deck while the sails and sailors fought and the lightning hooked down. The tropics seemed as unbelievable as a pineapple. The white Atlantic raised altars of water in front of our ship.

Pictures on street corners. Here the sign of Heron, Elephant, Ceiba Tree, or La Vieja — the old woman, horn-handed, hunched. To arrive at my quarters, turn right at the Shepherd, go the length of the Jaguar, pass up Cacao and Turtle, and come to the perfect courtyard on the street of La Rana, the Frog.

I *set up shop.* Young girls, their slender throats are small for the metal portrait stand. I move coiling hair, adjust nervous chins and the mothers, in their rows, stare at me. By the end of the day, I know I have taken their souls on my back and relieved them of suspicions for a century.

My companions. Down with fever, they should be safe with the padrecito. The servants are in town playing the lotteria. The ruins are mine. This afternoon I hauled the best

camera through the tangled paths, from one
falling staircase to the next. Centering
pyramids in the sun, I have never been so
happy or so careful.

Trying to get pictures. Knee-deep in rotting
water, bichos, the evil fevers, never let
go. The padre killed a sheep and placed the
hot skin against Cabot's swollen stomach until
the fleece grew cold. Again, again, the chunks
of heavy red wool, eight sheep more before
the fever passed and the swelling subsided.

Some mornings all I can do is get up. But
Bernaldo finds another site so we hobble
and hack through the day to get there. We
arrive, violent with chills, lucid with
pain, anxious to look at those fallen
stone faces and walk away as healthy men.

The pool. Thrown from the cliff above, a rock
shatters the pool. The thick jungle
fringe that reflects there shakes, as if
a norte — cold and violent — is blowing away
the upper air. It is quiet at the rim of
a cenote and dangerous. I hardly dare wonder
what magic is hidden in water.

LINDBERG COMES TO CANYON DE CHELLY

after Anne Axtel Morris

I was more concerned with weather.
A spring storm stranded me at Chinle
Where the canyon mouth widens to sandbanks
And cottonwoods bend toward flooding waters.
When the riverbed firmed enough,
I drove the aging Ford from bank to bank,
Aiming for the ribs of rock, skidding
Across quicksand, hands and wheel locked.
I traced the canyon's buff-colored inner
Flanks to come to our excavation camp.
Greeting me, Cook flapped his dirty white
Towel into a frantic bird, moved I thought
By flour, or mail, or the pure dusk's craziness
When crows threw themselves over the canyon rim
And circled down, never landing. Then up
On drafts to piñon trees, fibrous roots
Forcing out place holds in sheer rock.

As the car motor heaved to a stop, Cook
Pointed to the sky: "They came that way."

He flattened the letter under the lamp
And said "See, see." (They thanked me
For the camp's hospitality.)
And while ladling beans he told his story:
Early the morning I left, there was a first-heard
Bee-drone of a plane engine above de Chelly's
Lightning bolt of sky. Cook could not
Have been more surprised when Lindy and his bride
Cried down to the camp from two thousand feet,
Hours later to stand apparitional before the fire

Like old friends. They made long hikes
In wrong-heeled boots, but no complaints,
Found alcoves filled with broken tile, pots
Fat with dust. At night, blanket rolls helped
A tired head look across painted rock walls
That vault toward signal stars,
Then smell of sandstone, the animals'
Night calls and the canyon's long whisper.

Back on the rim they found the plane
(Landed expertly on a rocky strip,
Free of sage and piñon and cedar.
Only one small tear in the canvas,
Easily fixed). The wings dipped,
And Cook watched them disappear,
Past the rim, past the outstretched trees,
Swallowed into the same storm
That stranded me in Chinle.

Handing out his dented tin bowls
As if they held the sacrament — tools of trade
Now resonant and blessed by his guests —
Cook ended his story by looking at me.

A year passed. Tracing the headlines
In newspapers brought in overland
But only rarely, Cook felt
His way through their tragedy. While I,
Who only touched the shirt-sleeve of events
Second-hand, had to work to keep
Firm in mind the bright ruined faces
He saw in every dish he made.

YOUR APPLE TREE

Unexpectedly, our days were linked
by apples. Some mornings I lay

unwilling to wake on a quilt made
of yellows and greens. Light melted

across the torn window screen after
coming by way of the blossoming apple

that crowded your garden
in a good year or gently

marked the empty rows and drooping
vines during droughts.

One apple tree can fuel a whole
farm. Visiting, I'd find them heaped

in piles on the ground, in buckets
gathered carelessly abundant

on your porch, golden in jars as jelly
for toast, wrinkled in jars,

weathered, dried into slices
like kindling for the stomach.

In winter, the wait for summer apples.
In summer, the dream of winter appetite

for pies before stove fires.
I learned about apples that way, filching

from the overburdened tree before
our walks, discussions punctuated by

the brandished fruit, arguments ended by
that sharp familiar crack of first bite,

chittering birds chased by the cores,
the return, empty handed, to a chore.

The harvest gifts that I took home
were never as good, and hardy

apples withered in a bowl
because, less rural, life was too busy

for making pies, so I sliced
one batch to hang before my sink

to dry on a string. Their sweetness
drove flies mad. The string

sagged. That year we changed. I took
a trip and stayed away. In summer heat they

had no choice, the apples spoiled
before they dried. The link between such

days and these is a picture of your apple
tree fragrant in the wind and

the memory of that flight,
the string of rotting apples filling

with scent my abandoned house.

RETURN TO OAXACA

For years the trees have grown
To shade the square
And the bandstand's wrought iron curvature
Vaults there, and the paving stones settle,
Worn down by courting pairs.

Three years in ten I've visited:
The shoeshine boy grown older
Now owns an awning above a set of chairs.
The waitress in my favorite cafe still clears
The plates and glasses but has no memory
Of me, only of tables and who pays.

I am a gray pigeon, pompous,
Head cocked to see more clearly,
Tracking paper with minutia but aware
Of my tiny darkness, under trees
That dispense shade more widely
Year after year.

GYPSY DANCE IN PROGRESS IN A SUNLIT CORNER OF A COURTYARD OF SOUTHERN SERBIA

Imagine, first, the sunlight coming down,
As thick as sheaves, to the cold courtyard stones.
Imagine the smell of dust: spring being stomped
Into existence from the bones of winter
By a row of women who dance for their men
As you watch. Their hands, entwined, are draped
By colored scarves; their sweat gleams in the sun.
Imagine, if you are a man, the feel of coarse
Homespun under hand, and imagine, if you are a woman,
The heaviness of skirts, the way your feet move.

Tambourine, fife and fiddler, and a row
Of dancers before a row of watchers.
Pausing on that day, you see as much
Of the gypsy ways as you see of the women:
Draped, columnar, swaying gracefully in rows
As invisibly you walk out of the courtyard
Into the shadowy rooms of your own life.

GRASS: A MUSEUM

only two sides
jointed stems
sheathing leaves
flowers born in spikelets of bracts
narrow spear-shaped blades

when cut and sheaved
strong sour smell
when dried for winter
cow-skin smell

Everywhere it has a special name:
pampas, veldt, sedge, steppe.
We ask it to be boats. We ask it
to be watertight, to weave (baskets
to hold, blackbirds circling the lid),
to be rain hats, masks, oriental breast plates,
mats and mule straps. We ask it
to feed, to build, to welcome bowling
balls, to spring under lawn parties,
To ignore the dripping teacups, to give.

Men travel thousands of miles
To get more. Animals kneel to it.
Cities fight it with whips and edgers,
pushmower, powermower; farms fight it
with scythe and combine. Children
get lost in it and roll backwards.
Men paint their porches green.
They worry when it isn't there
and threaten when it is. A woman
brought rattlesnake grass to America
to grow in graveyards and alleyways.

In Africa eat lemon grass and be poor.
In Los Angeles have a rock garden and be bored.
Talk about grass at every party. Graze.

This valley, the Sacramento, is full
Of lush farms, of tomatoes, of tule
Grass bordering irrigation ditches,
Rattling anciently. Grass wins
the interiors of railroad tracks
and the flooring of abandoned houses.
On the low, fringing hills that entice
no one, grass flares through July, green,
Burning into a slow, autumnal yellow,
Serving no one, holding nothing. Gaze.

1225 B.C.

Egypt, during the plagues

There was sensible terror
When the river turned rank.
The ornamented birds
Faltered and fell motionless
In our nets.

We could not drink the water
For it spawned frogs
And the night air
Was full and loathsome
With their sounds.
The flies,
Like vats of black dye
Loosened into the sky,
Goaded the goats and cattle
That ran wild
In the wilting yellow fields.

The dead stank
While we sat inspecting
Our lives. All clean
Flesh festered and we seemed,
Ourselves, to be dying.
Some men walked unharmed
And claimed that sticks
Would turn to snakes
In their hands,
But I never saw it.

A great hail ruined the grain.
Darkness came. The city
Vibrated with laments
As parents ran into the streets
With their heavy dead,
Their dearest firstborn sons.
The days dawned expertly
On the empty land
And those still alive
Were greatly changed.
The waters cleared and the wind
Moved. But few of us knew
What wretched schemes
We had been so firmly caught in.

AWAKE EARLY ON TODOS SANTOS

After a Poem by Su Tung-p'o

Tropical air pushes through the front door
when I step out, expecting rain. Stars flood the sky.
Hoot owl and hanging bat dream the same dream;
cat slips through my legs and down the driveway.
It's early — lovers, ghosts of lovers — forget each other.
My memories and I amuse ourselves
while the day of the dead, creeps over the sky
and I pity smaller lights, lost into sunrise.
Morning air settles like a sweater, or skin.
The season passes quickly, in work and silence.
How long before it returns — a morning like this?
Those I love sleeping, traffic just beginning, mockingbird
mounting the highest rooftop, to heckle saints and stars.

ANGELS ON THE AMAZON

|6| Movie-(Adventure)** "Angel on the Amazon" 1948 George Brent, Vera Ralston. Weird story of an old woman who looks like a young girl because of an accident on the Amazon. (105 mins.)

This happened differently
where I traveled. Women
who were young looked old.
Their husbands looked like sons,
working with machete and arrows.

When a face emerged from jungle
one could only name it *spirit* or *witch*.
The pointed and broken underbrush,
the slick vines and runners,
created those thoughts or worse.

An abundance of sun marked off
each clearing. Cornfields
competed with the growing trees.
Old women, hoeing, smiled,
their smiles disturbing.

If they knew, they never told,
in their conspiracy of age,
of the miraculous accident
of youth. They wanted no miracle
or to be young again and sad.

Cooking fires sparked their eyes
while their smiles proclaimed
that youth had become another
dream, floating upon the river
as it took its slow course.

THE DISTANCE TO RHODES

In a house on the Gulf of Mexico,
she waits and watches birds fly
through the garden to the balcony wall.
They puff themselves up and begin
to mate. The male, colossal when he
comes to his love, calls: *the-greeks-
are-coming-the-greeks*. She listens,
impressed.

> The distance to Rhodes is immense.
> From there men left land
> and took to the sea, going beyond
> the statue and peninsula lights
> and the countless islands flowing past
> Greece. She lives on the last shore
> they would ever come to and tends
> tropic flowers and washes tiled halls.

When birds begin to strut and fly,
she craves other things and leans
toward the water, the falling waves.
When birds everywhere begin to mate,
she dreams.

CACHE CREEK

Late on a summer's day, all views were
   deceptive. The creek was as warm as the
   air upon it and the rock-tumbled water's
   roar like waves on a distant shore. The
   pool we swam in suddenly seemed limitless:
   the diving could never end or the arching
   and treading, the dolphin play. On one
   bank we slid, naked, across the crumbling
   rock and blue clay.
A sly time, the death of another summer,
   each minute was full of mineral sweetness
   and salty heat. When you put your fist
   through the clear plate of the pool,
   water foamed around us, lapping with
   smaller and smaller tongues.
The mystery of certain moments is how they
   end. At the edge of an ocean we would have
   paused and taken stock. On the banks of
   Cache Creek, we dried off, then went on.

CHICHICASTENANGO

The infinite inertia of bad hotels,
crackling kitchens, hard feet on hard tile,
the death of the pig in the morning wild,
whole days shaken by a dull church bell,

stench in the bathroom and dust on the floor,
beds gray with mattress, magazines, books,
awe-eyed daughters coming in for a look,
inebriate transistor player living next door,

not near the station, no water upstairs,
ankle-shaped cobbles, the greasy smell of night,
darkness abandoned to the 30 watt light,
motorcycles in the courtyard and men who stare.

The uncanny inertia of bad hotels,
the whole view shaken by the dull church bell,
stench in the mattress, dread on each floor,
inebriate transistor plays forever next door.

FINDINGS ON THE UNDERGROUND

There was a moment when the lights flashed out
As I traveled one morning to London
Past gardens and playing fields perfectly square
And green, fresh green awaiting the brush
Of rain. Endless stations flicked by, a brace
Of girders, names of tube stops colliding
Into each other, a smudge of letters:
West Harrow, Willesden Green, Baker Street.
And underground, in the vacuum between
The fixed platforms, darkness reminded me
Of night, of a dream I strained to remember.
My room before dawn could be any room,
But the dream that woke me seemed mine alone.
I closed my eyes in stillness, listening,
And tried to recapture some part of it.
Attacked then by weariness, I fell back,
And sleep took me quickly into morning.

Beyond Willesden Green the lights went on
Again. In the sudden glare, an older
Woman, mauve and pale, sat blinking, blinking.
Her occupation: to smooth her tan gloves,
To fold her hands just so. She blinked at me
So familiarly, faded as a whisper,
Like the night and the night's dream. How she watched
While I searched my memory for it, furrowed
My face to reflect her own. The station
Platforms passed, unexplored, going on and on.
Until my dream was smoothed away, until
I lost what I had mislaid the night before.
At Baker Street, when the doors hissed open,
She stepped out first, following a worn path
I could just discern into the city.

ON THE CHIHUAHUA-PACIFICO RAILWAY

The train comes to a twilight stop.
I am in my seat but looking out
at a girl who sits in her doorway.
They have turned a boxcar into a house
and placed it eight feet from the newer rails.
I notice a television in the interior
and dark figures watching the lighted screen:
such light almost holy in the depths
of an isolated highland valley.

No light but the last of the sun
picks out the orange and yellow and blue
of her dress. She looks at the train
as one looks at any familiar excess,
a long look, but she is visibly unimpressed.
And I am unable to signal in the slightest way,
being simply part of the darkness.
She dangles her shoes from her toe tips
off a porch without steps, then turns
toward the interior and the TV when my train,
as it must daily, pulls loudly away.

ARCHEOLOGIST'S WIDOW

Not a day passed, I didn't want you,
Not a city seen without a feeling of loss:
Marmaris, Rhodes, Heraklion.

I rarely talked, drank warm beer,
And chewed pistachios in small cafés.
I ran from places
Where men killed for women,
Where women killed men,
Where sons died in war, where parents
Ate their children, unaware.

I would rise at dawn
To watch the red-rimmed sea
From the deck of a slow-moving steamer,
Nothing before me, darkness behind,
Gray water.
I tried to send a message
Floating toward Gibraltar
But the bottle never reached
The open ocean.

One day I asked aloud
What you were doing
And you didn't answer.
For a moment, I couldn't remember
When you stood by me on the windy fields
Of Troy. So I returned to all our ancient cities
Alone, and slowly mended.
I learned one story worth repeating:
Artemesia, a queen,
Who didn't take a lover
Or eat her children

But who lost her lord,
Hired all the artists in the world
To build a bed of marble for Mausolus
Before they met again in death.

Thinking of this cured me,
Looking beyond the waters,
Alone in this very old world:
When my work is finished
How gladly I'll go to meet you.

IV. TO GO HOME

THE PEACE IN PEACE: AN EPITHALEMION

I hadn't expected to find it here
where my fingers feather your wrist in the quiet after work.
When I walk through a city you don't know
and tell reflecting windows and outdoor planters covered in first snow
all my easy secrets.
In the impossibility of phone calls — how to say
the same thing *again* ...

again is a poet's task. Each time more passionate
against the cold shoulders of cliché. Each time
more accurate if measured richly, as fabric unrolls from bolt
in organic yards the length of an embrace.
How many years it has taken
to arrive at this place: counting
out-loud appreciations room to room.
Cat takes off to blaze her way into the sunniest afternoon.
Dog curls around green chair rungs and smiles for our attention
in her dependable way.

Let the wide white blades of the ceiling fan
above this marriage bed
mix all the air for us that they can;
we'll share it, at rest,
and never feel done.

IN SUMMER

> ... *for he was just the mixture of ragamuffin and of genius which is dear to the heart of woman, who, however conventional in herself, loves the unexpected, the crooked, the bewildering.*
> — W. B. Yeats, *Mythologies*

I stand and water the plants at night
Listen to music, stand by the screened door,
Then let the cats out, the large one, the small one,
And follow them into the yard to dream.
I watch your face in every room, searching
For blue in your clear gray eyes and I
Tease my fingers on your wild chipped teeth
Figuring my fortune as your sighs
Grow long and light, leaving you asleep
In my arms. I might sing, if I knew
What to sing, for speech can be so hard.
And I would not stop before the moon cut
Its beveled outline into the night
And white moths filled the warm evening air.
As a cat waits for milk the whole morning,
I wait for your touch and your open gaze.
The persistent movements of stars,
The skill of your arms, the beckoning dawn
Are the unsteady dreams of my waking hours.

IN YOUR CHILDHOOD BEDROOM

I slipped under the comforter
into the deep ventricle of the family heart
that had labored, as all families labor,
circulating lifeblood
from your parents' room to each child's room
and back through the central hall
where a kerosene heater
flared out its years.
Where everyone held a humming
in the head and shared a shower,
where brown wood trimmed closets
held warnings and promises,
each person his and hers,
and all turned under synchronous blankets
to settle into another night.
Kept out by hope-thick walls, these same stars
folded across this same sky then
and character danced in small steps
through the narrow kitchen
into the ebb and flow
of screen door mornings.

I slept for many hours in that vein
of memory. I remembered
your memories in a sepia haze.
Which is to say, I couldn't remember them,
exactly or even imperfectly,
but overlay my own. We all
hope to keep hold of certain midnights
when we're poised to slide
into the secret of what our life meant
and what it might still mean.
Consider how a sister's hairbrush

balances next to a father's razor
while a mother's secrets fill a lower cupboard
of a shared sink, that holds a damp toothbrush
every year of our life. Fortune-telling
happens for real in the vanity mirror
onto which we layer the family face
in hot-breath and sometimes hot-temper,
avid with interest and wonder.

I should say I opened my eyes
as wide as I could but saw nothing
and heard nothing. Not the Atlantic — iron gray
under a winter cold spell two blocks away
tossing its hard spears toward the constellations.
Not the wind chimes that sounded
as sweet as the grapefruit
that bent tree branches
down like clumsy riddles
and gave back their surprise
when the sharp spoon gutted them
for our throaty pleasure. Not you, older
and mysteriously asleep
a familiar room away.

There could have been
a whole skein of your youth
tucked up like a ball of silken thread
that was shaken out
over me as I slept, a gossamer net
of want and have and have not
and need and see and don't forget,
filaments that played out with the furniture
the year you started your own life,

the year you slapped yourself free
like a baby with the cord rough cut
and went on your way.

I could feel, as I turned
face to pillow, as I closed my eyes
on everything I couldn't see,
that the current of sleep that claimed us
drifted through your parents' house
floating molecules from one room
to the next on the beat of many breaths
on the memory of talk,
and because of that, I could finally accept
that we all carry our own rooms — always —
centers of longing and dream —
transport these into every scene we enter.
That the storied heart is just that —
a very *very* good story,
not really a heroic muscle
locked in an unforgiving rib cage
but instead is a conflagration
set off by the deep sparks of some mad chemistry
on a tinder we're almost unaware of,
until we say — surprised ourselves — the obvious:
those impatiens are a beautiful red and growing well, or
that baby surely is the best baby that ever was —
this day is as clean and clear
and hopeful as any you or I will ever see.
It is each brain's citrus-sharp will that this life
is lived at all — over and over again,
however we choose to do it, ill or well.

THE WAY I REMEMBER

When he drops an egg into the enamel bowl,
my son pauses with clear-eyed precision —
asks about the cloudy cord between
the yolk and white — then pours in corn oil
and whisks left-handedly at this home remedy
for the dog's dry winter coat.
It's just how eggs are, I say,
keeping myself busy in the dawn of a new year.

        Mrs. Proby, in elementary,
gave my older sister Linda two banty hens
leftover from an improbable class project.
They lived in a box nest, laid brown eggs
the size of my five-year-old fist.
When she cracked eggs into the frying pan,
I heard Linda's certainty, a sound I was
raised with, determined and solid. My stomach
lurched as she ate, for I thought:
almost a chicken, almost a chicken,
as that incomprehensible word — unfertilized —
faded.

        I came to eggs more slowly —
an omelet in Garmish Partenkirchen.
Sausages hanging from dark rafters,
backpack left with any German fluency
by the fall-damp front door,
amid smoke and beer steins,
I looked across a rathskeller table
at my golden-haired young man,
wondering how I had gotten there —
omelet, oil-at-the-edges-taste, eggs branded
with their lace of brown on yellow

sliding into me like a handkerchief waves
at the bravely gullible.

        My daughter constructs egg salad,
sits on the high stool at the kitchen counter
dipping into it by spoonfuls. Hormones transform her
into someone I can and can't quite recognize,
part me, part my sister, but mostly herself,
with egg-smooth hands nearly the size of mine.

        Like her hands, the house,
painted eggshell white, is the color
of the unbleached duvet cover
on the new down quilt on the bed
where I waited often this winter. Oil and vinegar,
I said to you at the last, we don't mix but we made
a good undressing.

        The dog is a poised black question mark.
My son's fork finishes its manic tattoo,
egg and oil blended into a healthy tempera —
good enough to bind pigment to canvas —
surely this will gloss her coat.
He goes to her corner, sets the dish out,
white and yolk broken and folded,
each into each. She follows with interest
and with a dog's simple insight,
laps it all down quickly.

SLIGHT ARCHAIC

I love your silence,
the way you take my breath
and carve imperial cities
in the crown of my mouth.
The darkest corners
of my long limbs
pulse with lost kingdoms,
Africa waits within,
and the diamond waterfalls
you make from falling hair.

You improvise
on my lazy stomach
the steps of Persepolis
while palm fronds fill the bed
and the love of animals
lights our desert eyes:
pieces of night
within pieces of sky.

All the oldest cities array me
and I am glad to show you
the alleys full of ibis
and nightingales,
the rooftops crowded
with wry yellow monkeys,
the Mayan orchids,
the gardens of orchids.

We are fabulous beasts
both siren and satyr;
Atlantis is in our ears
and Babylon is built
where our hips touch.
We founder gracefully,
creatures charmed,
content as ancient moons
visible at dawn.

HOW ONE MAY MORNING LEADS TO ANOTHER

This cat is a sculpted vessel
awaiting morning's dust motes.
Gray and black stripes
and ember green eyes
house a lazy soul. His sister
disappeared two months ago,
into an early spring morning.
I've imagined a hawk's talons
and her answering intrepid snarl.

Mockingbird sets its mate as sentinel
on the garage corner
then screeches down recklessly.
Attacked, this aimless cat
moves belly down into monkey grass,
meows piercingly toward the front doors
and feathers in past me.
I watch the birds strafe
and swoop upwards
to the frond-cup on the cabbage palm
where they've cached their nest,
angled it precariously.

Each spring it's the same.
Something found, something lost.
Home cobbled and daubed
together and defended.
Predators and prey
moving at and away from each other
in their dance. Last night,
the old moon cut itself in half.
This morning, sunlight performs its rituals.
It's the first of May. Undecided,
and pushed low to earth
by an excess of birdsong,
the roused cat steals out again
toward the back fence.
The steady dog watches
to see what we'll do today.
In a moment, I'll shake my children
free from their nests and see.

MY CHILDREN HELP ME CUT MY HAIR

My son goes first, talks
up his normal informational storm in a far room
while she trims his growing-out surfer cut.
On the haircutter's couch, my daughter
worries about feathering or not feathering
long blonde hair, having teased her sixteen-year-old
boyfriend on the phone until he learns
to warn her not to cut hers short.
I page through magazines of zombie women,
scan the fake make-overs. I think: P*ineapples.*
Or *chow dogs. Artichokes and ferrets' nests.*
All alien-tinted; none of them wear glasses.

The day before in the B*ig* 10 T*ire* store,
getting a tire patched, in the *SuperSuds* getting
a truck wash, in *Wal-Mart*, purchasing endless sundries,
I stared at every head of hair. Thought:
Why do we even have hair? Decided:
Cut. Change. Do something.

Discouraged amid celebrity magazines' waif
young starlets. I decide on one, celebrated,
shaggy but wry,
walk back to the cutting room, and ask:
Can you make me look like her?
Joke and not joke. Desire is coin here. The haircutter
swallows her sweet incredulous smile
like it's clotted cream and she a sun-fed window cat:
We can try.

My daughter returns to life, feeling for the lost 1/4 inch.
My turn. First snip. Second snip. Long inches.
Bored, book in hand, my son wanders in.

Says: *oh my god*. Doesn't
remember me so in his short thirteen years.
Gets excited. Nervous. Honks forth
with a bottom-feeding teen's giggle. *Oh my god*,
rattles on a sealed door in the old house,
ejects three new blades from a dispenser
so I scold him on his way.
Intention: to stampede his sister
into a tension reducing fight.
We hear him retreat and repeat,
a diminishing echo of *my gods*.

Done. Hair apostrophes on the floor. Dark runes.
My daughter says it looks like a duck's butt. My son says
Oh my god. What will Dean say? because he
doesn't know what to say. My daughter
defends, deflates: *Be quiet. It looks great*.
The haircutter hands me my glasses, gasps, *I love it
what do you think?* She leans closer. *I can't
see*, I say. *You're in the mirror.*
 The back of my
head feels like a duck's butt. My hand pets
feathers. Chin lifts. I smile,
rise, walk, trip once on the uneven floors.
Tip well.
 I sail forth,
trailed by my squabbling goslings
whose attention has now drifted elsewhere.

FIRST MARRIAGE

The beer, the waiter, the check, the walk
Home through light and dark, the light
Now dark canal streets, oily water hitting
The houseboats and echoing under bridges.

Nearly two a.m., the bed upstairs
Begins to move. We listen and don't speak:
Too tired to sleep, too tired to wake,
Windows open as wide as the room.

People wander along the dim streets.
Car headlights strike them, on,
Then off, then the horn. Conversations
Float over the water, lift incoherently

Into our darkness. Passing light etches
Our room, then disappears across the window-
Sill. I don't hold you, outlined on the bed
And naked, silence touching us like a mouth.

WHEN YOU DRIVE AWAY

You drive home;
set your self aside
buckled in, on the truck
seat beside you.

From the edge
of a cool, fall evening
each star contributes
its single cold breath.

You light imagined lampposts
along the straight dark curve
to your house. Even now
each leaf is turning.

The garage is attended to,
swept into silence. Peace
is packed into habits
like tissue paper.

Your shoes like small doors
slam across the concrete
until you pause, hard
on the kitchen doorknob —

familiar hand, wart
on the first joint, left thumb
knuckle — familiar knob,
Phillips screw shaking slowly loose.

A lemon-pie wedge
of home light
is waiting, willing,
to fall upon you.

Your right shoulder shifts,
calls to your left shoulder,
before together you go ahead,
walk back in.

OMNIVORES

After being folded into his evening sleep,
Tait, age eight, returns to our bedroom,
says: "We're *un*divorced." Smiles.
I take a fancy to these unexpected words,
we *are* divorced but trying again, living together,
and I think, What if we all could "un" everything?

Undate the person who bored us, undo
certain words? Our affairs undone, no one hurt.
Maybe you never almost died
learning your allergy to wheat — still able to eat
French bread, drink beer, or, unmyopic — I could
hold a camera to my eyes, see clearly
at the steamroom and beach. We're
unrobbed: thief in Arequipa slipping passport
and money back into hip-pack on cafe chair.

We ask my father to forgo his
cancer, let him retire as planned and drive
an RV to see this warm, sleep-filled grandson,
who reminds me of him. Your mother,
not stroke-bound for five years and gone;
my mother an unsuicide, willing to face life
in glistening Santa Barbara sunlight. If my
untalkative heavy sister could be unfull, she might
not take the family past to heart. I'd give a lot,
if my children had never heard my sharpest voice.
Undivorced, I think, undead, unhurt, unsick.

But what would be lost in this tremendous
unwinding? My obsession with reading?
Your renewed interest in other foods.
Our need to have children? The blessing

in beginning again, glad we've come through,
married or not. "Undivorced," I say to Tait, "what an idea."
"Omnivore," he says, rubbing sleep from intent eyes,
"We're Omnivores," walks back into this night.

THE DIVORCE QUILT

We spread beneath us blue and white,
Pieced in octagonal flowers, like designs
In old floor tiles. We love and fade
Then wake to talk while tracing
Cotton stitching and random spots
That have begun to fray, whole going
To piece again but in a natural decay
Unlike the making. From woven bolts,
The pieces, cut, were trimmed and designed
To pass the evenings of many days.
You don't ask. Yet I tell you why I made
The quilt on which you rest.
And as I talk I think of folds of cotton
Flanneling the skin, of visitors
Pulling down coverings from a storage shelf,
Of picnics that weren't but might have been —
Children or masters by peasants in old movies
Tossed high in the blanket game.
And I remember the reveries I stitched in
As the blue, hand-dyed, rubbed off indigo
On my fingertips. I worked it
Through the years. Less in summer,
For gloom swept out with spring.
More in winter, as we fought the marriage.
The earth moved out the farthest distance
On its orbit ring, shortening days
And the quilt, lengthening, brought knowledge
Of what was ruined, made clear between my hands.
I snapped the last thread with my teeth,
Packed some few scraps, and Penelope reversed,
Finished my work and then was free.

Still listening, you help me fold this quilt away.

SESTINA: ON WHAT THEY REMEMBER

> *He remembers asking you for a date and he thinks*
> *he remembers that you almost laughed in his face,*
> *but of course that is what men remember whenever*
> *a woman simply doesn't want to go on a date.*
> — Letter from Hans

He remembers a woman
she can hardly imagine,
asked a question with an air
so indistinct it's pure molecules. Home
then was a cat and a cottage she would
not show him. She had dreams

of language and movement. She would dream
in that cottage. Call another man
who had stopped her one chill wood-
spiced evening, saying "Imagine
those stars, for someone that's home,"
familiar of cosmos with his disturbing air.

Face it, men made her daft, gulp for air,
laugh all humid night, sweat, dream,
sex a trekking out, an escape from home.
Years later she can't retrieve that woman
or his name, lost, alliterative, eyes imagining
hers and she, if she could, would …

Why, she thinks, she would,
Why not? She *has* traveled. Here white air
stacks stories high into imagined
sky-scrapers and slant dagger of heron dreams
her into more distinguishable memory — that woman,
she thinks, brings him home,

cat feigns disinterest, home,
sharp exclamations of hot wood-
fire. The Sierras loom, lie woman-like
inland from the coast of memory's airs,
salt skin eases them into their dreams.
Recasting a net of past, she imagines

her young rebellions, an inland sea just imagined,
poured onto paper, at that old desk, in that small home,
retrieves the moment as in dreams.
The man asks his question. She would
transform her answer across a lifetime of air,
from the present, understand that man

and that woman, imagine
them, sculpt air into desire, holding home
safely within, would dream again, even those imperfect
                              dreams.

WHY MEN SNORE

When young they run fast
and coats fill with feathers and leaves.

In hunting camps follow fathers
into days of wood smoke. Raise ladders

to paint fumes all summer; carry odds and ends
into cellars and attics. They endure

the perfumes of women, chalk on cues,
locker room on shirts and socks.

If roused from their dens of bedrooms,
their lungs fill with the old air

of inflated balls, stale dust of construction sites.
Foam of first beer teases each capillary

and interior cavities wash in adrenaline fear.
Fathers, mothers fall away, friends compete,

and bodies are need. They consume
each day whatever is offered.

To exist is to be invulnerable,
or healthy. They agree to mow lawns;

fill chainsaws with gasoline. They breathe
harder into their age, enter an unexpected distance.

Early morning, the world reappears
from a dew-heavy tent flap

in its foolish beauty, exactly
where it once disappeared.

Safe from the hunter, too full to hunt,
bears amble into brush, curl and twitch for days.

Steady snows blanket rank coats.
And shelter is built of impossible sound.

MEN WHO LEAVE

Some men it seems are not content to live
The life that they have made. They leave the wife
And kids, a house they find constrictive,
Their boring work and small-time social strife.
One day in spring, in Fred's Cafe, they follow
An inner urging and push away the food
Then start the Lincoln and pull out slowly
From the curb. If asked, they'd say they needed room
And time to sort things out. Fred shakes his head
And calms the wife; the kids want Cokes and whine.
They don't return, the men who leave. Instead,
We meet them ten years farther down the line
Nursing their discontent: new wife, new brood,
More inner demons and the mortgage due.

MEN WHO TRAVEL TOWARD THEMSELVES

The socket-wrenching pivot, eager foot
on another road, long-abstinent legs on another bus,
the gray bands of days and nights passing
during hours of near sleep, radio marimba,
rapid as memory, playing the sleepy skull.
Do you wonder how young daughters like old wives
come to curl the same way in strange beds?

Eyes, they could be any woman's eyes,
important if you could come to know them
this clear morning by a foggy ridge of deep mountains.
Lightning purples the mouth of coming darkness,
adobe stairways of grain mount hillsides.
Wheels you hardly trust, speed you past
the dream shattered lava cities with their histories
of the weapons of revolution. In young couples
traveling forever, you meet the flat obedient maps
of some past life. Dawns seen alone now:
cold candles, shadows of day, a straining heart.

Rough drinks in a warm bar ignite sadness
like tallow. A bonfire beads your face
with red sweat, all your jobs, whispers, days, births,
your hands, your voice, explorations and endearments
burst like firecrackers
        at five a.m. on the cobblestone eyelid.

The moon is familiar to you, her wanderer.
She sees you move foot by foot
across an obscure globe. These are the prophesies of fog
— white dreams will always pierce the window
      where you sleep
— days will become a sad mirror of night
      as people you have never known
           shake your hand and say "welcome, welcome home."

LATER IN LIFE

When later in life you meet as old friends,
After being in the world a number of years,
Alone and distant, out of contact, you tend

To be apprehensive and choose an austere
Demeanor for meeting. A well known cafe
Leads you into endless insincerities.

Awful to watch a friend gone to seed play
With his food as gluttonous desires
Mobilize his face. His balding pate

Makes you rub your worn hands. His talk inspires
Boredom, nothing more. For his part, he stares
In disbelief at your dress. A lack of desire,

A pass of the celery, and the past is ignored
And repressed. You talk of the present, coups
And fires, the topics you never before

Required, when love was your daily news
And sustenance came from intimate talk
And passion enacted. But now you are through.

With a squeaking of chairs you rise and walk
Out to the street. You are nothing alike?
Too confused to part, you stand and gawk

While cabs tug at the curb like stray kites.

BLACK SHEEP

I think of the twenty-five years I might have been home.
When the high winds blew the big limb down and crushed the fence
but missed our children who were watching, I was alone facing west
on the road deciding: Spokane or Cheyenne? The late night
when you walked on that muddy road by the barn, old water
frozen into fists of ice, the blue-star quilt around your shoulders,
thinking of the next day's deliveries, I was telling your secrets
to Angie Lee in The Palace, in Bismarck, ND, and thinking of ice that
grows between the double doors, the way it could be chipped and
heaved off a drunken porch. Coffee thrown from my mug freezes
as it falls. Each deck shuffled, folds again into these thin hands.

GILLIAN ALONE

> "*I am not depressed by my depression
> if you know what I mean.*"
> — Rebecca West

Gillian at Home

Gillian at the moment she really understands. The reclining chair where he rests, mountain of male, white T-shirt stretched thin, like a screen door across a shaded front porch. Children, playing outside, breed static, entering into and underlining the argument.

Gillian's TV

I look gray, factual, unwise. But I watch near their dinner table; they gnaw at manners, hold pungent arguments, smile like meatloaf and canned peas, casseroles with yellow cheese. When the children finish and go outside, the parents shift size, equalize. His bulk in commerce with her fury, they're paired like shadow and shadow-maker, like salt and pepper shaker. Distinct, indispensable, is the tension they save for each other.

Gillian's Changes

Gillian as a fragrant, appalling, husky dairy cow, high bony back shanks, folds of skin falling groundward. Her once lovely pelt sports black and white Holstein spots, splotched Rorschachs of her times.

Gillian as a darkened room in which the ungirdled flesh
 of women feels comfortable.
She's a patio at night with water making worried noises.
She's the stars clicking outward, under remote control.
Her galaxy turns audibly.

Four for Gillian
> Gillian would never choose to be by herself.
> Gillian would never abandon her children at an interstate highway rest stop.
> Gillian would never tell you the truth even if you guessed it.
> Gillian *chooses* to be by herself, and the furies she is sure will chase her, harridans with permanent wave rollers, don't arrive on time. It is a sunny day where Gillian lives; for the first moment in years, colors seem auspicious and not too bright and not too wanton and not too untrustworthy.

Into and Out of Gillian
> Soap and German goblets and Japanese brocades, self-help books and trashy scenic paintings — heavy with green heavy with yellow — and sweetly sour red wine on Sunday, late, and seersucker bathing suits and empty lipstick tubes, go into Gillian.
> Wishes and cheese casseroles, some 1950s acceptable behavior for unknown neighbors, some late night terror — blankets that smell pink and leaden at the same time — and a way of reading any print — signs, contracts, cereal boxes, menus, church bulletins, inoculation and report cards, billboards, and TV evangelists' phone numbers repeated twice — and a way of sitting very very still, disallowing sharp hand movements, before the opinions of doctors, come out of Gillian.

Post Gillian
> She sees the stars as street lamps. She sees the earth's bulk as a householder's joke. She stretches up on tiptoes to see her children, her children's children, her children's children's children, her children's children's children's children. She surprises.

Portrait of Gillian
> There is no picture. There is no picture. The set is blank. The moment is edited by memory, rigid, unyielding, rigid, unyielding, and unwise.

WHY SING OF A FATHER UNATHLETIC

Why sing of a father unathletic
Blessed with daughters only and a heart condition
That kept him from the flattened playing fields
Of a small suburban division,
Who would watch the Dodgers on television
Through sweet spring days while we
Walked our stiff-armed dolls on laundered lawns
And, wide-eyed, watched our mother
Make her desperate motions to him: not to strain.
Who knows what thoughts sped through him
When young Drysdale pitched, reviving
The sandlots of our father's youth —
Some midwest moment: a sultry summer,
Girls in long shorts, his bat connecting
With Tommy Jenkins' fast pitch.

Why sing? Only that he bore it well
And loved his row of gainly daughters
In pigtails almost as much as he loved baseball.
One summer night he walked down
To the local field: one team was one man short.
He stepped up to the plate as if his chair
Had buckled suddenly and sprung him free.
Experimental the swing, dredged up from memory.
Two of my sisters, talking, missed the thing,
The slow response, but heard it connect
And came running, as we all did, to the boy
Who fielded the hit with his stomach
And fell back in the bland dust, stunned
And out of breath. Our father kneeled beside him,
One hand to his breast. As the boy heaved
And gasped, our father did the same, lost
And terrified by the knowledge of that game.

TO START MY FATHER'S HEART

Start what I know can be started.
Start his lawn mower. Let it kick into my
      nostrils the smell of oil and cut grass.
      Let its throbbing pulse in my ears.
In the kitchen fill the dishwasher with the sound
      of plates. Start it for him. Let him hear its
      comforting spurt and trickle; its hour of humming
      like a contented stomach.
Restart the cuckoo clock when he forgets. Pull
      down the counterweights and the heavy
      bronze pine cones begin to fall. Check the cuckoo
      in its cottage, its painted breast. Count the minutes
      between chimings.
In bed, start to listen. I must be prepared.
      Because my father's heart started so many years ago
      at his unimaginable birth. Because a heart is a machine.
      When I hear the pounding the pounding the pounding
      the pounding, I rise from my bed. Help him with medicine,
      with my hand on his chest.
When it starts, kiss good-night. Give one last
      knock for luck on the cuckoo's nest.
      And go back to bed.

HOUSE/HOME

Architectures of thought. Think of
Skulls. Think of learning that everything
can be fixed. Wood rots. Insects' march.
Paint covers and then water
seeps through again. Good bones
allow for good revisions. Layers of plaster
and patience, but both can be overlaid.
Corners. Plumb and true, sprung
and sagging. Overarching
or low, looming ceilings. Containment.
Walls that frame a view. Personal
perspectives. Seeing family members
come into a lighted hallway.
Lights flickering off. Sounds muted,
then springing sharply from shadows.

> Bodies, warm, uncurling into spring
> mornings. A teenager drooping across
> a dusty bed, reading a book
> that rests on the floor. A dog
> rubbing along the front wall's baseboard,
> painting it grimy with her tail. Silence
> behind a door. Bedroom a cave. Kitchen
> a hearth. Shared secrets. Blood relations.
> Affiliations and alignments. Some
> sense of destiny and delight. Also
> rage at limits. Echoes of ancestries.
> Knowing, years later, where every
> light switch is in the dark.

Speculations and samples. Swatches
and choices. Adjustment. Compromise. It's
not done like that here. It's only in our dreams.

In our minds. It's work-free and full of grace.
Fine-grained woods without a scratch.
Thick carpets and inlay, material wealth,
lengths of patterned silk and dust motes
in a gold tinted light. Well-mannered
inhabitants. Veneer of everything. Lines
of borrowed symmetry. The pool that never leaks.
The child who never slams the door. A heart
that never hurts. Dangerous absence
of sentiment and satiety.

        Walking the perimeter, feeling safe
        and embattled. Curled around hopes.
        Scents of showering, must, and toast.
        The plans that never grew up. Green
        houseplant drooping in a shiny brick-red
        bowl. Clatter of should haves. Napping
        after a restless night, distant lawnmower,
        like unneeded punctuation. Interrogation
        of ceiling fans. Old clothes. Dressing up
        to go out in a sudden mirror. The world
        rain-wet across the brown lawn.

The door shut. Key tossed
from one hand into another. Check stubs.
County and city offices. Cardboard
schemes. New plans. Restlessness.
Clean lines. Moving on.

The aftertaste of a birthday cake. A standing
army of photographs. Wide-eyed blink
of a two-colored-eye cat, sunning herself
and humming threats at the unseeable
bird feeder behind thin curtain slats.
Your hand. My arm. Books in confetti stacks,
read, waiting to be read.

FEVER BOUQUET

I'm defrosting the last of last summer's pesto —
homegrown basil and Romano cheese,
garlic with Georgia pecans — watching
Florida light flood a February evening
while my daughter's fever spikes, 103 degrees
and worrisome. She says "Oh god it hurts"
with a too quiet, twelve-year-old's voice.
I place the cold washcloth at her forehead,
raise her shirt to check the rash. Her breast buds
slow me; I was thinking of other things.
A small shock, though we've been expecting
them together for months and weeks.
She sighs with her croupy chest and turns
in her body heat, slipping back toward childhood,
labored heartbeats held between lush, chapping lips.
Two days until Valentines and all the valentines
I collected in the past could dance on the head
of a pin for what they have taught me about how
to help with the betwixt and betweens — the almost
grown up, the almost well, the not quite but soon-to-be
springs. The freezer finally is empty. Outside, brown
winter grass waits to serve up its latent seeds.
I drop capellini into boiling water. A room away,
her breath evens and she sleeps. I sniff
green and garlic, pour heart-red wine. I eat.

FOR MY DAUGHTER ON HER GLASSES

It's this predictably surprising thing we have done:
Formed her face, a set of hands, that sensibility, from mud
Almost it seems; creation myths read in Arizona sun,
Said breath of life blows from walking gods, buds
Into a Laughing Girl. She sets her glasses down like this,
Like me, And asks "Do I look okay?" I compare
Her open face, without interpretation and now adrift
When she looks at me this way. It's afternoon, we are
Mirrored in her bedroom window. (She mirrors us in all senses.)
"With two nearsighted parents ..." says this cautious advocate,
"I like you best, either way." Half 9, half squinted into 19, she senses
My finesse, but dreamy eyes still ask, "Who am I?" She can hate
Parents who brought her unrequested genetic plan into being,
Or grin, put glasses back, hold hands a short time more with me.

THE DENSITY OF WHITE

I see her at one of the basins,
standing on her pants, a shirt
tied by the arms at her waist.
She dips to the sink, twists
a cloth and raises an arm like water.
She bathes, legs wide for support
on white tiles, the cloth
winding around and in.

I stare toward the space above
and below her breasts, curving from point
to point with my eyes, with my eyes
repeat. She lets me watch while rose light
falls from high windows.

Without talking, dry and drain.
The sucking water wakes me. I walk
to my basin behind her back —
it is beading with crystal beads.
From her thighs beads crash
onto white tiles.

I watch in the mirror as she leaves.
After she leaves,
there is nothing to watch.

IN THE WEDDING BARN

There are only a few things we could tell you
by dropping them into this champagne-flute afternoon
that tapers toward the end of September.
Wisdom, we might point out
accumulates in small events,
when wide-mouth bass nibble at water's surface;
when deer glide down slope
to watch a family perform its ceremonies;
when bats glint in corridors of pine and fir
while rabbits tease each other toward the edges
of the lake of evening.

Cleared month after month like a child's slate,
the moon's familiar face encourages you
to forgive and forget what matters least,
to make room for the moments
that hold you together — rebirths,
journeys, the promises of seasons —
each a translation, each a transformation.

As you learn how generation speaks to generation
in the sure lines of lineage, hear centuries
communicate, one to the other, as the stars with earth,
we would remind you, most often, simply to listen —
when your lover takes your hand,
when winds rise in storms,
when mornings seem to hold back
and tempt you to rush forward too quickly.

Wait. And consider why you came here,
up the grassy slopes of expectations,
into the hotter flames of appetite
which fill each dancing moment, kindled

and rekindled with the energy you give back to it.
Never forget how the quartet of contentment —
generosity, passion, kindness, courage —
performed all day long, how your guests,

held smiles up like little mirrors
and reflected the rightness of your affections.

Before life's glass is completely full —
harvested, seasoned, poured, and savored —
recall the time you spent here, as rich
as the ceremonious dust motes.
When you return in such a way,
you'll discover what you have saved, what is left,
what is best in all you have done;
each anniversary asks
that you slide back large wooden doors
so sunlight falls onto the foundations
and barn swallows sketch their greetings
across the consecrated landscape of your hearts.

AT EIGHTEEN

the house consumes its silences. Front door
sticks. Maddened, you toe the echoing brass
kick plate, swing purse like a conspirator,
plow uneven red brick walkways in tall and terrible
sandals. Low slung jeans underline emerald
belly button ring, deep in its mysterious nest.
Right now blonde hair. Right now,
tattoo of acne at neck and forehead,
panther's crouch, involuntary mortal breath of damn,
god damn. At the street corner, other people's cars,
their reflecting windows. Your cash register says empty.
Your boss says you're late one last time.
In the mall of sleep, row houses fill with dream families,
not one of them your own. In a museum you've yet to enter —
Portrait of Young Woman by Window — sun outlines hair,
thin folded fingers, blue smile blooms in secret. You have
changed your life. Each day passes, faster, slower,
exacting, and almost without redemption.

STORM

    for Morgan

I walk outside into the applause of the palm trees.
Wind we rarely have is as warm as the dog's breath
and just as jumpy. I skip into the night,
leave behind your careful observation: "you're laughing
because you're sad" — and my answer — "I'm still sad
but I'm really laughing. Your dad, his girlfriend,
are eating grouper and spinach soup?"
(and I'm signing you up for soccer and dancing
wild dumb dancing with you, your brother,
to an old Talking Heads song on your teenagers'
radio station).
        "This is my life," I told the clouds
      massed behind the neighbor's house this evening
      when we ran outside to gape at the billowing sunset.
      "That one's Mt. Shasta" you said, and I said, "That one's
      Mt. Lassen" though we had left them miles behind on our
      summer vacation.
        I don't walk too far, my arms windmilling
and stretching into the warm tropical deep night air,
before I feel the first drop fall. The dog scents into late
summer grasses so green they're blacker than the night
these last weeks of August heat. Then another drop.
We continue, trot, walk, the hot smell of rural asphalt
blotting up first water like tears. I snort at the dog
like a wild horse. I freeze like a deer in the brights
of some car coming home down a cross-street.

I wave my crazy fronds, and the rain grows thicker,
and my tennis shoes squeak out the storm, steady,
colder, downpour now. I'm filled with electrical tension
like the usual lightning that's stuck, unmoving, in darkness
to the south. Since it's missing, I walk farther than I might —
I hoot for the owl, let the dog pull me along
like a bat on a leash. She's sure she can outrun
these waters. Scents have turned so heavy
we wick the midnight in, then shake ourselves
into the silent, waiting, sleeping house.

ON SHELTERS

Highway patrols tell motorists not to feed gray alligators
that float toward road margins during spring floods.

There are far too many cages and keepers
for true discomfort. Red birds in my garden

feel hedged in by blue weather. Avian engineering
mated them. They bring forth polka-dotted eggs

near cat-patrolled lawns. When local droughts drive me
to water, bird showers drip from greenish-yellow palm fronds,

delighting lesser doves who concentrate on the word *invisible*
as clear water falls. The lovely syllables of *paloma* aside, doves

act as thick as the plain and placid tourists feeding reptiles
spare pancakes, then pulling into traffic on a sunny collision course

with their manifest destiny. If I sound insufferable
don't stop me. I'm the kind who latches the warped garden gate

after my black dog escapes. Raw tongue wagging in truce,
she tears off gaily with my unspoken shout.

MOORS AND CHRISTIANS — A SESTINA

All in all, I prefer black beans.
My children won't touch enchiladas
with olives and onions and cheese
even when they see the ingredients go in. Chilies
and Tabasco, forget them. Ketchup on tacos
and the most flawless white rice.

Some Sundays I make my arroz
and think of past travels. Mash fríjoles
and remember — fiery handmade tacocitos
from stands on one street corner, enchiladas
of intestines spiced with whole chilies
but seldom, in Merida, any fresh queso.

Behold these bricks of supermarket cheese
and the body bags of rice
that I don't have to sieve. Chilies
with pre-labeled powers of hot. Beans
and a product called Beano for farts. Enchiladas
in gooey rows and assembly-line tacos.

I heat up some lard, scooped from a box. Tacos
sizzle. I light two painted Saint's candles. Queso
blanco crumbles, white and salt. Enchiladas
burn my fingers and I plunge them in arroz
the color of Christmas trees. Then fríjoles —
when I mash them, the children watch. Chilies

come in eight foot plastic lengths. Chili
holiday lights and just a memory of tacos
filled with nopales. Once, in Patscuaro, ollas of beans
on the fire and not a nibble of cheese.

Why the stones in my landlady's rice
could break teeth. But, ah, enchiladas! —

little pockets of flavor — fresh enchiladas.
In the Tehuantepec market, only chilies
it seemed — to break the heat, with heat. Arroz
con pollo handed in through bus windows. Tacos
too, though I regretted those later. Imported quesos
for the rich and for the rest, more frijoles.

Here at home, it's Sunday. I heat beans and enchiladas
in the microwave. Sprinkle with cheese and chili.
Next week I'll make black beans and rice, Negros y Christianos.

HERE IN THE NEW WORLD

I'm making Norwegian meatballs for the second
time in my life, for elementary school — fourth grade's
write-about-your-cultural-heritage-week; this year

for my son, the youngest. I know now to make the meat-
balls smaller and cook them longer. Three years ago,
my daughter watched hawk-steady over spitting oil,

then made a face of adult-food dismay
when she tried her first. I've changed too
in these years (while fourth grade continued on

like an established dream — "write a one page report
on an interesting ancestor"). I've moved from
Viking-rage to Newfoundland peace, ex-husband fallen

away at last with the bitter dregs our years' poor harvests.
Today, my children go through their paces — Shetland ponies
wickering their excitements into green coastal fogs.

Simmering in pure cream, this meal is totally incorrect —
I've bound pork with beef, with egg, potatoes, and bread —
calories enough to fuel a northern winter. The black dog

slumps before the hot stove, enjoying our fragrant day dreams.
Friends have returned to Florida for solstice. And soon we'll all
return, from eonic darkness, like a carefully hummed song,

the one I've spent years growing used to. I hear it when we
eat together — fish and fowl — sour and spice and sweet — pass each
plate and toss our stories into the bone-dish of the future.

IQ AND AGE

In the elementary school library
      where I'm waiting for you to grow up
      are short tables and tangerine chairs
      is a burglar-plundered model railroad
      in its smashed Plexiglas case
      is a five-foot dinosaur, scale modeled,
      but too friendly to instruct
      are unopened books, wedding-mint pale.
Edge to edge waits this enormity of words
      for serious readers
      who sound out a story
      in thin flutes of air.
Your voice high and sweet
      or is it under prepared?
      You are friendly and forthright
      earn the test-giver's thanks
      and a treat. He writes
      and records. Who scores?
Down the hallway out
      you run to double front doors,
      see darkness, see light,
      before you push the right way
      for us both, and move into yourself.

A TEACHER MYSELF, I CONSIDER MY CHILDREN'S SCHOOLS

Which teach about STDs by state mandate
Then write up the young girls on a field trip
Who buy condoms — to see —
From a vending machine
In an actual restroom,

My children's schools
Have not yet been visited
By a rifle-wielding student
Who was sent home yesterday
For coming to school with a rifle
But any day this could be,

My children's schools
Ask for my signed parental permission form
So one class may present to another class
Their performance of *Macbeth*, including
The bad words,

My children's schools
Have gotten our attention —
By making us tuck in our shirts and wear belts,
By being generous with test score celebrations,
By reminding us not to read ahead
In assigned books before the rest of us get there.
We do it anyway,
Including the bad words.

Read our books.
Hold our breath
As we watch TV news
That someday
May include us
Despite us.

HOUSE BUILDING

Starts out slab simple, a ship's deck worth
of dumb concrete surfs across the face
of the lot, former cattle pasture cleared
of kudzu and lighthouse-tall live oak.
Not near gulf waters but tinged with storm nature
from egrets and gulls who hitch drafts
to cumulous along the near lake.

The team of carpenters with golden weightroom thighs
wrestle up the fabricated rafters
one radio-long day then disappear to secret bars.

Sci-fi spiders on clay smelling stilts,
plasterers revel in splat and ooze, smooth
swampy layers, erase a sense of constructedness,
seams of plasterboard.

Electrician's cat's cradle of misdirection
secretes switches behind doors,
links fans to wrong sockets, at last
connects the home's life source,
galvanic surge one sultry night
when the whole shell veers into definition.

Floor boards go in at midnight,
whine of saw within breeze of a humid, rising storm.
Painters pause to listen on giddy chemical
highs, then stripe out former misdirection,
mark sunrise walls, trim the eyes. Before long,
walks and driveways set, fragrant sod arrives.

Children once swallowed whole in that skeleton frame
chase more slowly when walls solidify,

clatter aboard this ship of fabrication,
slam new doors. They cast themselves into
the hide-and-seek of habitation,

shudder with growth,
and sleep the first night
peaceably at anchor — new moon
framed in the high arch window
with its single star.

EARLY MORNING MUSE

The same coffee made the same way, the drill of the grinder,
    the flavors of memory.
White blinds raised in a regimental salute.
This reflecting black window.
City siren surges to the foreground,
        imagined emergency room parking lot,
    raw doors slamming.

Dog collar hits the food bowl; paws break leaves on the red-tiled porch
    as she stretches, ungainly, to gnaw her tail.

The pink light begins.
Car speakers pulse against air for blocks;
        stock boy prowls toward his job.
During the cat's piteous and ornate serenade,
        one unbalanced section of the newspaper
    falls from the kitchen table two rooms away.

Stifled snores. Pillow shield sleeper from the day's near surface.
The taste of the second cup,
    milk cooler on the rim, chiffon skin.

Fingertips poised over prey.
As the yellow light shawls shoulders, the words drag you deeper
    with their audible kiss.

Lover. For the life of you. Here's how you'll render up
your daily tithe of attention.

SELF-PORTRAIT: TAIT

The night before the fifth-grade Christmas holiday concert,
my son lays out his good clothes: new navy khaki pants,
new white shirt, and a silly but durable bright green tie
that has hung its slack noose in his closet for years
only revived at times like this, for his sister to knot
in her teenage fists and say — *if you don't like how i do it,
you do it* — when he twists under her dominate assistance.

Tonight, he spreads the blue slacks on the rug below
his bed, smoothes each leg. Then the white dress shirt
is placed above, and tucked into the waist. One arm
of the shirt flung out to the right like the happy success
he dreams off-key about, one arm of the shirt folded,
elbow-angled on the left to the waist. Like the serious
family member he is, he understands more than I'd like
of absence, separation, the complex calculations of love.

He takes the tie, figures of skiers across its green face
to mock our Florida snowlessness, and runs it around
the neck, beneath the button-downs, and practices his knots.
As I call out his bedtime numbers, he places socks in shoes
and shoes at the bottom of the slacks and then calls me in:
I pause at the doorway in order not to step on the portrait
he's drawn: a boy waiting to be slipped into, to be given tomorrow's
breath, a waving figure that eases into a night of rest.

PRETEEN

I sit
on my daughter's bed
where sun cuts like a breast-bone
across her dust of shoes,
fancy soap, books and beads,
rank tossed sheets

where she rests each night on ten year's growth
of bears, a bat, tiger, pig, possum —
lumpy fur-covered bed of nails —
and demands another hug
or pushes away my bending sweep
to straighten her corn straws of hair,
and snail tracks of saliva,

where she curls like the cat who scratches
slowly, under one ear, one leg,
looks at her with his dark-wide eyes
and she looks back,
blinks, goes out like the light,
as I stroke electricity
from his tortoise hairs,
tell him:

let's always remember this.

TO GO HOME

Think first of places that aren't home —
>   the open cooler in a midnight Suwannee Swifty;
>   coins in the mall fountain with their sad dull light;
>   any bar with its three stony figures,
>   counter always tacky, neon lights
>   branding each forehead.

To go home, plumb narratives of hot breath, heavy hands,
>   and sheets — if you remember sheets-
>   -gaudy lemon and lime striped flannel
>   or humiliating race cars inherited from brothers.
>   Cool crisp and white sheets stretched
>   tight and straight.

As you resurrect shared meals, hear voices
>   from another room high and loud or indecipherable —
>   radio on at the end of the hall, the DJ's voice familiar
>   but just lost to memory, TV on in an empty kitchen,
>   empty dinette chairs at attention.

Maintain a cinematic eye for the impossible. Remember
>   a late summer afternoon, light in live oaks,
>   someone rocking on a porch, the blisters
>   of liquid on an iced tea glass. Are bats *at home*
>   as they hang upside down in gunny sacks
>   in this swayback barn?

Maybe you played ball in street traffic, liberated radios,
>   broke headlights. Maybe you learned to
>   hunt while the fathers were telling drunk stories
>   by firelight, tried to stick around when the mothers
>   gathered for dessert and shared their coded tales
>   of the body's flux and flow.

Maybe you built forts; ate mud, paste, and chalk,
    floated in a canoe as if in an afterlife.

Maybe you danced past midnight in the windowless
    basement disco when the fire that consumed
    Luisa and Raul forced you breathless into dawn.

Maybe you're at home when the trailer screen bangs
    in the wind that pokes little dust devils
    up the empty road.

When the railroad shakes the studio— turntable hiccups,
    stylus tiptoes across two bands— look out
    and notice the woman on the stoop across the street
    three floors down, patting each of her boxes
    with the Braille of dispossession as the new tenants
    move aside, then in.

My dog is at home when I am; she likes the safety
    of her metal crate, cool and echoing, an ancestral cave,
    musty and ripe with her scent. She settles
    until she is as comfortable as a heartbeat,
    rests for hours, legs tucked, tongue hanging loose
    in a dream-grin of enviable trust.

My sisters, older, built homes, bought homes,
    became experts at real estate— farm land
    and suburban— lived in factual constructions
    long before I did. I'm known for two brown and tan
    batiks, a Japanese silver birth cup,
    and a collection of Mexican saints
    who always move with me.

To go home, turn three times before sleep,
> make a nest in memory. Was the bureau against
> the left living room wall? Did we keep diapers
> in the top drawer and a shotgun and shells
> in the bottom? Who called his name? How did she
> answer? What was the sound of the piano
> you never learned to play?

Undertake that dream where you float over the landscape —
> dressed? naked? — and looking down.

Hopscotch over a multitude of school buildings,
> a courthouse, police precinct, teen center,
> grocery store whose aisles get smaller
> every year, local dump filled with possibilities
> or despair.

Finally,
> land
>> safely.

Tell us where.

RELATIVES RELATIVES

Atlantic Beach, Florida

Beyond
the white-washed air
of the empty family beach house
doves send hollow greetings down high-tide streets.
A Dalmatian tows a coffee-holding owner homewards;
                                            a lab-mutt tries
to dune-drag his toward tideline where upscale houses
                                             have piggybacked
onto the beachfront. Their jutting, upstart stories shade
                                          the low-slung first settlers, bow
before the jeep-tread-marked shingle where waves
                                          continue a January agitation.
Count steps down a sand-filled lane. Listen to the creak
                                    of the wire gate
and stare at red painted steps that raise you
to the second floor porch,
feted by generations of seashells, collected
and set along the ceiling shelf, filling one glass lamp
below its crooked, stained shade. In a listing dresser with one
missing drawer, a replica of an antique gun;
                                    in the kitchen with bent-walled
cabinets, a china rack painted orange catches the empty gaze
                                    of unused appliances.
There's the salt shaker collection — bee hives and cows —
                                      as useless as palm fronds
in storm winds. Details collide. Water drains tangy with sulfur;
                                      rag-rugs nestle
against wooden floorboards like pets. Predictable and pleasing,
cabin furniture with broad arms, with tan indestructible pads,
buoys you up. A ceramic chicken dispenses twine
for packages that are never wrapped,

her snipping scissors hidden
behind her immobile, fanned-out tail.
Reader's Digest Best Loved Books pairs *My Friend Flicka*
with Edgar Allen Poe in a hand-built bookcase in a hand-built closet.
Bifocal eyeglasses wink from a littered shelf.
                                        Cousins and grandchildren
line thin board walls in freeze-frame versions of their past lives.
                                        Heater-vents
pulse with an oddly recirculated air. Memory-ghosts
gather like prehistoric dust motes,
float from afghans crocheted
in motley colors by Aunt Grace whose eyes
no longer could see what her fingers could feel.
Alert now, tease the tip of a broken metronome. Recall
that story of Uncle Austin — how he brought home the wild raccoon
from one of the Ten Thousand Islands, unthinkingly,
                                        because he was young,
and how it got loose and holed up spitting in the bedroom closet.
The bathroom infinitesimal! How could a family of six
dance their lives clean here? All youthful then, before parchment
fingers placed photos of brother by brother,
and sister by sister on the closed Whitney
keyboard. Sepia grandparents guard the rooms. Green
trim screens and slatted window blinds — white paint — years thick —
glazes all with stiff dignity. One more time,
the moon hoists itself above this wide
Atlantic, which cradles arrivals,
which washes each
next morning
free.

AUTOBIOGRAPHY

My lives look like subway cars, colliding along the rails in the dark
when electricity blows and passengers lean precariously forward.
Someone falls into someone's lap. A man with a suitcase lurches
away from his safe handhold; the lady with the white purse laughs.

My husbands meet in the back room in the TV glow, the game is
in a final inning, they jostle for remote control. They decide
it is easier to be friends than to be with me. They take up viola
and amphetamines, marijuana and Go games, computers
and credit cards; they share their *whens*.

My children hold a family reunion on a soccer field,
get in the players' way, run hot with memories,
start shouting matches from sideline to sideline. They stand
face to face in exacting symmetry. They claim: *you never* and *you always*,
trail picnic trash of torn paper, of matches and apology.

My lovers leave the house early, walk the neighborhood in the dark.
They head west but forget to wait for me. Those who stay
lift the lid on a cauldron that reheats on the stove.
My dogs howl in barbershop harmony. The cats stalk off.
They have always known it would be this way.

My sisters meet my lives in the corners of their municipalities.
They say *really*? And *fine*. My brothers arm-wrestle my lives,
waiting for surf on a pacific ocean where they've gone to get away
from their own lives. I should remind you — my lives are giving
themselves a surprise birthday party — everyone is invited.

My lives line up like clothes on a clothesline. A shirt billows
out in grass-sweet-smelling dry sun. A skirt hangs inanimate
in drizzle rain. My lives dream as wind rises, bath towel flapping
and solitary. Why, even now, my lives snap off the line
and fly into the space between this place and my other lives.

V. OUR SHORT GREEN LIVES

THE CULTIVATION OF MIND

I don't know much about birds
although they stick in the trees of my best

mind. A cardinal searching for food
can shake me up with his red flares

and, if unready, I depend on his workaday
wife. Her determined dull plumage won't

lead to mislongings. Amid litanies of perennials:
I trowel up a border and set down potted

roots to luxurious unwind. This thought excites,
this scene — me running amuck, unleashing exotic

lily, and olive: Red Japanese maple shivering
in bird light: Blowing, drought resistant, sincere

leaves: ginkgo, silver dollar eucalyptus, also ash.
Does the coin of creation nurture anything

more weird than a spotted owl, at night, sweeping
low over our toy-town citizenry? I say: Set

cultivated beside free, transplant the uprooted
ghostly wetland. I think: Welcome, the red-robed

officiant, and the one-legged egret of idea. How
our fluted, our hollow-winged wishes, hallow horticultural

tinkering: That breathes life, frees dulled longing,
fills an Einsteinian hole, so we actually live:

Oh — our short green lives!

THE RED CLEARING

Sleeper, if I return to your hands tonight let me tell them these stories, crave my hips and legs. The histories of my flanks are histories where you live. You are afraid of drowning so I drag you down. You are afraid so I tell you not to be. I say your hands are as holy as death and I open your eyes with my eyes. Forget the familiar rages, the poor small angers. Here we are dressed like emperors, hierophants, knaves. Everything abandoned by sunlight is alive at night. The sheets are crimson, the ceiling raven. The darkness is a cloud from the garden. Our life is the naming of animals, our rest a desert story, our sleep a dark wood, our redemption a witch's tale. Our sacrament makes all months one day and crowds the heavens with stars, with the dust of warriors, with the wisdom of old women. We traverse the universe in a many-armed boat. We freeze like statues and burn like gods. If I run across the moon, cross the sun to meet me. If I risk my life to guess a secret, run afoul of your family. If I give up a kingdom, steal a crown. If I change into a tree, conquer the last continent at once. We meet at the sea, minions behind, tributes rolling in like dolphins on foam, miracles finished, tents raised, the colors of the world tying up the sky, the stern faces of heroes ringing the campfire, the risks of love dancing like children, dreamers weaving together in a long garland. With your hands my body is fish-bright, maidish, eager. If I return tonight let me tell you these stories. Sleeper, listen to my hips, the histories of these flanks are histories where you live.

MID-PASSAGE

April night,
a mockingbird nestling
serenades the full moon
as if it were the sun —
sings unskilled embroideries
to the counterpoint
of a hoot-owl's profundo —
pulls melodic threads out —
then stitches and restitches,
high and low,
throws each trill
against my screened window.

Outside,
under night's spotlight,
I admire the bird's young energies.
My soul!
look how the saps of spring
are moving
under this attentive round moon.

BRAIN TECTONICS

1.
I might have mentioned the wonder of mouths. When I opened my lips, hieroglyphics slipped out. Large symbols cut the air like rock. Were these mine or my parents' words? Are the pockets of the brain filled with that fabled language making device or just recycle centers where the crew slams in at dusk, empties its wasteland full of rinsed tin cans into aluminum airs? Does imitation precede mutation? Will my daughter's consonants — that she practices on her brother's drumset of determined ears — boomerang back as her own or as distant echo of my years? Engraved profile, archaic mouth, temple of lips: sound, listen, hear.

2.
I wanted to check the photograph. The one I hired taken because I couldn't look to a familiar lens and smile. A turn of the century superstition that the camera would capture the too gregarious soul. I thought if I looked irresolute into those sights I'd be unraveled.

Even the studio's lens delves some truths, from behind the eyes, in a fugitive light. I wanted to check the photograph. All day. See if, not soulless, I'd spread the sign of self too firmly across my self, signal flag upon a barricade of days. I'll stop now. I have to see.

3.
Young, I bent my father's voice to my own purposes, military directives, loose laughing ownership of world, wanderlust, although always with my own rare timid backpack. Still, I used affirmative and imperative like twin bolts of lightning flung down on life's forehead, waiting to spring forth.

Older, bending myself to children, knees surprising varieties of previously unexamined floors, I fill my lungs with lost power, tune questions, ask — *why, why not, please, please not* — or damn my stylized lot to hell. Sometimes like a hailstorm, sadness grows larger, colder, each time a wish hurtles into the titanic stratosphere.

Sure flatten corn, clear the room, collapse. But melt is so sad and too final. The various floors littered with uncapsuled words fuel family battles between rare bone borders, the wide awake and fearful skull.

4.

If she was lost would I want her back? Would there be a word that would bait a hook to bring her out to the ether of memory, twisting on the line, clanging great scales of rainbow armor? Would she be as small as I was then, or has she grown, twinned seed in a Jonah stomach, that queasy feeling just her turning over in my sleep? My sleep her sleep?

Maybe an uncanny Magritte monster, half holding to the sea, half beached on the strand, torpedo shaped torso, hair a net, legs a shadow, face someone's I always immediately forget.

I remember singing in water. I remember sitting under lamplight. I remember surfacing where dawn soothes a horizon. I remember, against current, under breakers, praising, foolish, almost glad to leave alone. Willfully lost, would she take me back or would I just lead on?

INLAND SEAS

If there was anything you wanted
This is where you would find it
On the slow drive
Where highways lap together
Like tongues and light dances
At the end of each frayed strip
Or at night when you realize
Hell is *you*, driving forever
Into a sleepy, black-quilt of a sky,
Radio fuzzing out on the best words,
Everyone in the car asleep.

If there was a time when you wanted
Desires to come easily
Like the passions of dead essayists,
Like the hopes of the sentimental
And the fury of the shopworn,
It would be here, where you have been driving
For the last few days.
For the last few years
You have been making this approach
And now you find
That the flatlands are flatter
Than you ever imagined.
Brooding hills that circle the plain
Are smooth in the sun and sharp in the shadows.
Colors shimmer as if they will not
Trust you. The road disappears
Under your feet, but you keep moving
And looking at the blue, liquid body
That rests ahead. You imagine it

And it becomes real
>	Soft breakers on the black sand,
>	Inlets of brackish weeds,
>	Water ringing around thin legs
>	Of slow motion swamp birds,
>	Clouds piling up as if stuck
>	In a drawing and the water,
>	Pleasantly baleful, welcoming,
>	Yet just unfriendly enough.

And you know, not suddenly, that this
Is just what you wanted. You imagine it,
It becomes real, as the heavy sky
Begins to unroll with a slow challenge.

RAGE AND GRATITUDE ARE HUNGER'S ANGELS

About face in your face;
ribs heaving in and out;
measured increments
of importance; body puffed
like a hooded snake;
puff-fish; fist sound;
mouth with no sound;
standing up straighter;
making little out of less:

perhaps warmth of mahogany
or violin shop full of exotic woods —
zebra, ebony, bird's eye maple;
breath on the neck;
body flushed with recognition;
blood's red;
lingering taste of oak in wines;
imprecise but diligent clapping;
blessing given from arms spread
at cliff's edge, ocean listening:

imagine plants that grow downward
in darkness; imagine bursting
from a cave's grip into too much light;
tightened shoulder's inward arc;
bargaining — *this* for just *this*;
texture of ribs textures of desire;
life so fully lived it's tired enough
to stay awake all night;
raptors above deserted highways,

eyes turned toward creatures
that move, creatures that
just stopped moving:

there's no angel in the house
unless you count the pleasant confines
of emptiness,
sudden music upswelling,
no angels beyond accurate adjustments
of a near miss;
leash that unrolls enough
but not too much;
any foolish sacrament of earned oblivion;
smell of cool night at high altitudes,
the distance between these cool, cool stars.

IN MY CUPS

      1.

Step stool to a sink
as a child.
Morning water
pours through the fleshy net
of my fingers —

clear fish
that slip into the drain's
unblinking darkness,
and swim toward the coast.

Sand in my hair   in my swim suit   in my sun sweat,
my heels dance drum
and dimple the tan sheets of the shore.

As each hollow refills,
a fish of salty light thrashes
then stills.

      2.

Unbalanced half way through night
the fountain of dreams
cascades from cheek
to collarbone:

snakes from armpit
to below breasts' folds:

seeps into space at stomach
where your spine backs
toward my belly's warm spoon:

trickles down our tributary legs
to toes.

We stir the hot lake
at the bottom of our bed.

    3.

I invite air
through cheeks' bellows,
into lung's stronghold,
parcel it out again
like airy fool's gold
dispersed in the clatter of being
in the glitter of each exhalation.

Turning afternoon's hard corner,
my hands grail
the cold red sunset
carry it inside
to the forge of evening,
burnish it with a slurry of breath.

     4.

The body semaphores
with shapes. Concave. Convex.
An opening always also a closing.

Eye empties its catch of the day
into nerves. Stomach's hydrology
is not to be spoken.

As slivers under skin
dissolve or turn to scar,
all we've had and held,
mark us
and testify.

The seven worn paths into skull's plainsong cell

depend on finger tips —
inverted sensitive cups —
balanced perfectly —
without hinges —
seamed tight — forming

hand's articulate nests
so I can feel, say, hold.

THE OTHER ONE

You are the one
For whom life hasn't
Stacked up colliding tragedies
As when someone called Richard
Dies in an Andean train accident —
1978, 1988, or 1998, it never matters.
You are the one just walking into
Or stepping out of the action.
You are never Richard,
Haunted-eyed, arm in arm
With a group of laughing friends
As seen in the last photo still extant
Taken in Belizean island sunlight
On that day about which
Everyone there said, "They already knew."
Later. You are the anonymous
Other one, neither stern-jawed suicide
Nor collapsing victim.
No cloroquine resistant malaria dupe,
No plane crash survivor
Disappearing in the wild Antipodes.
You have the peculiar
Sensation of walking firmly
Down the center aisle of an empty
Church: dog-furred red carpet
And stained light from the high glass.
You expect traffic noise
And a head-turning congregation
But neither is ever seen
From your particular angle.
You walk this way, often
Puzzled, no clearer than anyone else
As to why fate trounces here

And blesses there, but sure
If fate's schema exists
Your part is the simple bewildered norm
By which the fantastically outrageous
And the merely tragic passes.

PART OF THINGS

Again is part of things. Women turn yams into dinner, heavy
   wooden pestles drop into wooden mortars; feet press down
   long corridors, dull gongs of escape; the tongue-tip touches
   its wet bed, carefully, gropes toward the root of headaches;
   five a.m. storm silenced, but waves pound the seawall; the
   body pounded from inside, takes its proper form, heartbeats
   stretching skin across the drum of the rib cage; food fools
   the body with its fuel, as rain finds tin roofs. Sleep doesn't
   come fast enough — or at all. Magnolias form from brass
   and steel, armadillo burrows under hot evening air, railroad
   tracks smell like warmed chocolate: this repeated, wind-up
   action of dreams makes waking life almost familiar.

A HEART WITH EYES, AN EMPTY DRESS, A BOAT MADE OF DIRT

for L.H.

She cuts crow photographs from magazines.
Not for presence but for absence,
for their black shapes speaking from darkness

without judging darkness. Feathers highlighted in Hades
with blues, greens, and purples. Crows — smaller than ravens;
ravens — larger than crows. Both, keen-eyed and voluble,

tumble into her portfolio, knock each other about,
arrive on canvas like pleasing whispers of madness.
Constructive work to be done: church sculpted from cow skin,

embroidered heart, filled with gray hair. Each installation
awaits incarnation: ghost dress above a boat made of dirt,
cloth wrapped cats, and black silhouette upon black silhouette.

Glossy magazine, broken open at table, shows how one bird
made a riotous snow angel: traces of feathers etched
into snow dust. Presence in absence. Rude inspiration

as crow flapped away, buoyant, shrieking.

MY RELIGIOUS DEVELOPMENT:
A PARADELLE FOR JEREMY

In childhood taken to Methodist church, but wary of hypocrisy.
In childhood taken to Methodist church, but wary of hypocrisy.
Became a searcher of landscapes and faces,
                                      weathers and geographies
Became a searcher of landscapes and faces,
                                      weathers and geographies.
But taken to geographies of hypocrisy, in wary weathers became
a searcher of faces and landscapes of Methodist childhood
                                 and church

I sought stories in all good books, waxed tender with secrets.
I sought stories in all good books, waxed tender with secrets
and mysteries, drew faith from solid ground underfoot,
                                        like any Capricorn.
And mysteries, drew faith from solid ground underfoot,
                                        like any Capricorn.
Like all Capricorns, I sought faith from any book's secrets,
                               drew mysteries,
waxed with stories, tender underfoot, solid in good ground.

Currently, at peace as agnostic, deist, woman-Whitmanesque too.
Currently, at peace as agnostic, deist, woman-Whitmanesque too.
Age creates its own sleep, sobering waves of silence and faith.
Age creates its own sleep, sobering waves of silence and faith.
Currently, faith creates its own, sobering, too-Whitmanesque space.
Woman of silence, waves, and sleep. An age as deist, agnostic peace.

Landscapes of waxed weather when childhood searcher creates
from geographies of Methodist hypocrisy. But wary faces too
like any sobering stories of age. In secrets, I sought space
and peace and silence and sleep and drew solid faith in all its mysteries.
Then as to own faith, when Whitmanesque ground taken tender
underfoot: currently a Capricorn, deist woman, at books.

A SHORT INTRODUCTION TO PHOBIAS

Acaraphobia — Fear of Small Insects
Forty-seven beetles in the swimming-pool skimmer
all trying to survive — but who is counting?

Agoraphobia — Fear of Public or Open Spaces
My mother looked stunned in fresh sunlight; after a lifetime,
I find out she's right.

Ailurophobia — Fear of Cats
At night, the whisk of giant tails, pampas grass
against stucco walls.

Belonephobia — Fear of Sharp Objects
He plunges his tongue deeply into my heart;
neither of us ever stops talking.

Claustrophobia — Fear of Enclosed Spaces
Sand falls through bleached white bone:
tightness of cow's eye-socket, locked room of my ribcage.

Monophobia — Fear of Being Alone
Old science fiction movie — skin-diving the day the Bomb drops
— phone rings across an empty city.

Sitophobia — Fear of Food
A dream where my feet take root, a hand reaches to harvest —
my green scream.

Ocholophobia — Fear of crowds
A Sunday soccer match in San Miguel —
caught the wrong way against the one-way turnstile.

Pterygophobia — Fear of Flying
Fiercely, I imagine a city bus has just taken off so I ring the bell
signaling — this is my stop,
this is my stop.

THE SHAMANS

If spirits inhabit the earth,
Men must dive down to them,
Swim through rocks,
Shed their skins,
And fall into the fires.

Our world is left
With the skins.
They are the blanket
That covers the bed,
Plants that fill the dirt,
Cloud enveloping blue air,
And reflections
That gild the seas.

Skins of sunlight
Hang between mountains
And skins of birds
Lace the morning.

These men steal something
From us all and carry it
Deep into the earth.
The smiles women save
For small children
Are taken.
The scented limbs
Of trees are taken.
The white bone curve
Of whales, the rare
Smell of tropics,

The color of all flowers,
The sound of winter
Ice breaking again
Are all taken.

The endless arms of light
Go down with them.
Do they know we wait
Alone on the rim of the world
Like women watching
A dangerous sea
For anyone to return?
Do they know, these spirits,
We wait for the answers
To clothe us and the hot fires
Stirred by our divers
To ascend?

GLASS HOUSES

> All families build a Glass House, open to the world and live inside it; these houses are our inheritance. My family's house has the burden of being real as well. It needs to be heated and have its taxes paid.
> — Dominique Vellay

Light falls through glass blocks in sheets of gardenia-white, moves in fragrant waves across our skin. We sit at dinner suspended in conversations of sharp edges and heat. * We walked in Cadaques in the heat to find Dali's house: tilted blocks of Mediterranean stucco. After, conversation at the cafe, priest presiding in white collar — two women friends, wine, bread — sitting relaxed in God's house of sea air above the waves. * The swimming pool throws hot waves of reflections onto her imagination. She rises from lost sleep, sits to tell the stories. Drawn tan curtains don't block this encroaching light, gull-white and delivering its seaweed stench of tumbled conversations. * Childhood, distant conversations by adults, touching your hair, waving at you through windows, pointing to white shirts and blouses, complaining about heat and rain, holding a finger to lips, blocking exits, telling you, "this room, this. Now Sit." * We escape the mall of destination only to sit on cold marble steps in another conversation. Tour bus down the block. Teenagers disgorging in waves. Eyes shaded against the heat of what can be said, difficult, and monument-white. * The perfect house: gallery white walls and alcoves. Sit and admire the views. No heat needed, sun pouring in through glass like conversations late at night. Someone important waves and leaves, you follow outside, and down the block. * Memory is a set of blocks, square and white. Magnolia blooming now in waves. Conversation's broad green leaves, white blossoms, appear over night at certain houses, up and down the block.

GHOSTS' STORY

One day the house felt a heat in its loins —
old oil furnace flaring by itself into sudden heat —
and suddenly its owners looked in mirrors and felt their wrists.
A mirroring light filled corners and opened up rooms
where, once, love had been made lightly and long, and now
again, a roomy quilt folded with more care, a sweetness
settling on eggs and toast, daily cares less care-filled,
and up and down stairs children settling more easily
into their rules. The house glowed with attention. Downstairs
in the living room, conversation ruled again, daily events were
related like poems, plain speech was important. Time surged
through the circuits and light bulbs. Plain, unrelated
events began to appear related.
                                     In the century-old basement, lovers'
stories hurried to important conclusion, urgent stories, in letters,
pressed for safety behind the insulation, letter by letter,
words ignited and the whole house fed
on this now tangible mystery.

THREE P.M.

That hour when your earnest self meets
your hopeful self; the hour that melts

with sunlight and a faint scent of cocktails
all over the state: hour of cards

dropping from hands, of waking from set dreams:
ones where you win, you float, you drive

away care from the linens of the longest days.
In that hour, sun cuts itself into parcels, drops

through louvered windows; in that hour, clothes
sink like flags to the floor while custom

beckons you to an evening of promises: try
waking, try walking into the liquid traces

of night where stars blot away day's promises
and fill your deck with raw flourish of persons

just like you: forged by siesta in the recharged
batteries of the afternoon: the ways birds roost

in leafy shadows and hold their chatter
before any dawn.

FRANKENSTEIN

You are silt.

You are ice that melts
in the pyramidal mountains
and floats the rich skin
of valleys to this place.

You are acres of birth,
brown and sun-warmed, reflecting
the sky in thin shades of gold,
hiding the gold
and all the shattered gems
that form the sands.

You fragment everything
and change into something else.

You are love, growing
a picture of a face from memory.

You are the memory of all faces,
as many as the painted sands.

You are old,
primeval, the killer
and beginner of love
who rises half-sadly from the seas.

You are clay that dries
into strange shapes.
All shapes, sands, all memories
vibrate through you.

You are earth, a crucible, where cold
creatures sink gratefully
into the heavy and forgiving body.

FORTUNE

Iced, this numbs;
heated and sugared —
salves. Sweat gathers,
beads roll down.

Bitter Green
or English Earl,
stuffy, dull.
Each leaf —

once dry as dust —
wicks up wetness,
a kind of lust.
It drowns.

Steep it long,
breathe in, taste dusk
in a small blue
china cup.

I toast my year
just gone. My life
may be lost, found,
in foolish dregs.

Tea leaves line
the delicate cup.

ADDRESSING THE BODY

At night I address the body, carefully,
As when backing down from a position
Held years too long. I go on at length
Explaining how such as we can be friends.
After all, we were friends once, buying
New shoes, jungle-print skirts, and blue
Mascara because, at the time, it suited.
Surely, remembering our heyday, an attempt
At regular exercise, a short trip, an affair,
Couldn't be misconstrued by one who once took
Such activities as absolute good. Thus,
I address the body, as mere caretaker to garden
Or housekeeper to house, and retire,
Knowing it will hold me shamelessly
Begging our old dreams until dawn.

AFTER EPIPHANY

Your mail still reads from left
To right, and the typewriter needs
Your fingers. When you try to return
To *it*, repairing an old oak rocker,
Already down on your hands
And knees, the hard wood laughs,
The ceiling nods, and the hammer
Splits the sudden air. No, not there.

Dreams don't turn inside out
And illuminate. Breakfast still
Has to be made, and all nature rushes
Hurriedly on its way past your window.

Yesterday, everything lay down
And you forgave it. You had
An opinion on every plant
And an errand for every animal.
Today, you try to collect yourself
In every corner of every room,
Saying, "Was it here, here?"

TEACHING THE TRICK NEW DOGS: A PHRENOLOGIST DREAMS

Driving through an overheated town behind the red
sports car, I see two silver heads of hair, one tonsured,
one blowing like an angel's feathers, until motionless, at stoplight,
each feather falls. We all turn right, and my fingers curl
around the leather-scent of this eternal steering wheel.

**

I'm given a jaw and trace its harp-bold curve, jutting bone
beneath lively skin, strut to the skull's dome, bridge
and hinge. My hands hurry on, hover in benediction, make soft
passes above the lodestone brain: remembering, once, we lifted
one out — wrinkled walnut, labyrinth, erosion on a hillside of thought.

**

I can craft continents on the shoreline your hair gives
up to skin, drift, tectonic, across warm scalp. Summer brown.
Braille of intentions. I try to understand the electricity
of every thought. At my touch you turn, offering continents and
continents; I strum my passion down, soft rain across the globe.

**

I encounter a row of patients, lined up, each in a conversation
with themselves: in a firehat, a hard-hat, motorcycle, pith
and diving helmets. I tap with frustration across each shell,
pry at smoothness and mine for secrets. Merry New Year!
they chime out when touched. Outside, all the engines idle.

**

Trading a card shark a lesson or two, I find his forehead
full and tremulous under hand, knead the upper vertebrae,
loop my indexes around frontal lobes; his hands, flat on the table
begin to move, deal a royal flush, pause, deal a full house:
two specialists, our fingers spark and smoke until we stop.

**

There is nothing lonelier: this cavity full of space and memory.
I rub my brow and ignore messages, distract myself with
knees and elbows, miss each ear's horny rim. There is no business
like the present. No path to my closed door. I decide to take up
stars and sextants, transgress a freeway margin,
pass into some future

with these rusty hands.

DEATH

Take this grave matter
of death.
Examine him with sterile
hospital mirrors.
Prod him. Pinch
his hairy grinning buttocks.
Pass a lighted candle
behind his eyes and blind him.
See all his faces and carefully
count each decayed finger
as it falls with a thud
on your heart's shoulders,
as he leers with a maggot's breath
from your father's sickbed.

Treat him worse
than he treats your own.
Know him better than your mother,
more intimately than your Christ.
Suck up his earth hoggish smell.
This plague.
This fatty perfumed sweet release
with theater masks. Fool.
Jingling. Knelling. Multi-cornered hat
he sweeps in a low lusty bow before you.
Mockery.
Know him well enough.
Push your fist down his throat
every time you meet.
Leave him
languishing on a bed of nails.

Sulk thorny lover.
Travesty of hope.
Know him well enough
to forget.
Or kiss his ass forever
and wake each morning
to a penny-bright new hell.

CLOTHES CLOSET

> *There were thirty almost identical dark suits from Savile Row, each with money in the waistcoat pocket, ready for tipping.*
> — Victoria Glendinning, *Rebecca West: A Life*

It's never like cleaning out your own closet
the faded flowered 60s shirt floating forth
like a self-induced leftover drug dream;
the very tight blue jeans (from before
the first pregnancy that even then didn't fit right);
the ties, wide and flaccid, as conservative
as the tongues of businessmen in piano bars;
the stiff white baby shoes polished by sentiment
to a high gloss while nut tough children
burst from shirts and pants, ornery
chrysalis', the worn rags of childhood
trailing behind as indecipherable messages;
or *the* T-shirt, more holes than material
a faded red less appealing than menstrual blood
grass stained and dog-ripped and Other beloved.
Bagging it up for the dead is a matter of no hope
and much repetition: mother's twenty-four pair
of fire sale shoes, permutations from the same last
in unwearable colors. Belts for dresses that don't exist
and beltless dresses without animating form,
not even the anger of diet or the madness
of consumption. This closet full of clothes
doesn't dance behind closed doors, doesn't shout
to be used by The Deserving, doesn't do much
but stare back: hose in shoes, cuffs in pockets, tips
in waistcoat, hats, bags, and handkerchiefs ready
for that last well-dressed trip to the cemetery.

THE FIRST MAN

> *In only one of Daguerre's pictures does a man appear, by chance a pedestrian on the boulevard held still during most of the image.*
> — B. Newhall

Trees edge the boulevard.
Emptiness settles around the man.
He stands on a street corner
One leg raised for a shoeshine.
I tell you, the place is deserted
Not even a shoeshine boy attached
To his foot. See, in the photograph,
A boulevard that only *feels* as full
As Paris should to be Paris.
Lost, the carriage, the horse,
Sounds of carriages and horses,
Shouts, fights, newspaper
Boys, schoolboys and shoppers.
Lost, the shoeshiner,
Who somewhere still labors
With glittering black invisible strokes.

WATER'S NIGHT

> *You are sad, all at once, like a voyage.*
> — Neruda

Waiting as you turn in sleep, thinking, ankles
in water, days spent dredging the shore, heat
burning away the outer skin. Waiting for you
to wake, even now I remember the rhymes of old
waves and feel like a high cliff. Even now
I am pushing a boat across a sea as large
as the wide brown Amazon. Once you asked me
"Doesn't it seem crazy that we all die?"

I am not surprised at a gull with feathers of sun,
at a whale with fins of water, at a ship with
a hull of souls or a raft of dreams pulled on
by dolphins. "I am not surprised by death."

Here in the exact center of our world, on this wide
beach, in this velvet water, I dive and hear voices.
Bubbles break around my haloing hair. The circles
of the world look simple under water. The face of
death looks like a song. Under water you can cry
and go unnoticed and swim back greedily toward
the black sand beaches.

I am not surprised. Sleep is the color of water,
your face the color of seas. I gather messages
and spin out weeds. Shells pile around my ears
and every time you stray farther into your sleep.
I turn, count strands of current, and float
until dawn.

MY LAST DOOR

— after a Georgia O'Keeffe painting of that title

Let my last door open into the light of late spring.
May it be shadowed with the announcements of those who walked
    into darkness before me — right foot disappearing first,
    body leaning into the unknown, trailing hand making mostly
    mysterious gestures: *I'm all right* or *come along*; *it's what* I *thought*
    or *it's not what* I *thought*.
If my last door does not accept spring, I'll offer a fall's stark light
    on the hand-hewn wood lintel where abstract snowfall casts
    cool gray shadows.

Let my last door be a familiar shape, but slightly reworked: perhaps
    an entrance, perhaps an exit, its pattern fabricated, as words
    are fabricated, to let me explore the shoulder-wide rectangle
    of experience I claim as my life.
Let me walk up close and peer in long. Let me decide I don't need
    to look. Let me stay where I am a while longer in my small
    corner of the courtyard, intent on giving pleasure as fast as I
    take pleasure in this dusty sunlight.
Let a star shine through my last door.
Let me ride above the clouds and know somewhere, below, my last
    door is waiting, as someone beyond the door, is waiting.
Let my animals, children, and friends, pour their lives across the
    paving stones I cross to find my last door.
Let the flowers lay themselves down if they wish beside my plain
    and simple door. Petals will glow like a color wheel and the
    scent of honeysuckle, rose, and orange blossom will provide
    the toll of any crossing.
Through the last door, may my lover and I hold hands as long as
    we care to, as long as we can, neither sure which side the
    other is on, nor aware of when or where each of us has gone.

Let my last door be the one I chose to call my last — let me not
go back on my words but accept them when they arrive
to greet me.

Let every bird I have ever admired — like the mockingbird and
sassy stellar jay, the anhinga and rare quetzal — contribute
to the happy indifferent cacophony from a perch above my
last door.

Let me hang my worst impulses on a sliver of moon and sail it into
the sky. Let the bony skull of my urgencies rise like the sun
over high walls before I approach.

Let me regret and accept yet still turn onto the pathway toward
this, my last door.

There is no curtain on my last door. There is no space to stand in
or on. My last door will be neither wood nor wall, neither all I
imagine nor less than I can comprehend.

My last door must be imagined now, so that all the days it takes
me to find it, to figure it, to fashion it, are given over to its
attention, its understanding, and its praise.

COMING BACK

> *I have taught myself joy, over and over again. It's not such a wide gulf to cross, then, from survival to poetry.*
> — Barbara Kingsolver

I lie down with you and in this old way
reconnect to my body: thighs and calves
that buckle with robust cramps. Small bruises
outline hip-bones. These are fragile territories.
I learn to cradle desire, like saucer
to cup, like a summer lizard pressed close
to sun-white stucco walls (who pushes
up and scutters off). I lie down with you,
run our experiments from lip to lip.
The moon brushes the shallows of my back
with benevolence. I float into this.
Stars in the solar plexus (a friend once
gave me that line as a gift). I lie down
with you, for a blue moon, an orbit's bliss.
Then, reassembled and faintly happy,
I'm prepared to face my next tragedy.

ON ORANGE

Let me always remember orange pleasures
as I suck life from the smile-slices
left in this afternoon's refrigerator
from my son's morning soccer game
where twelve boys and girls
fingered them up greedily from the bowl
flung jagged peels on the bench then ran back;
I bent, picked and tossed rinds
into a trashcan, watched their world move
across muddied green grass.

I eat one, then another slice
at the sink. Such greediness overcomes me
I go faint with memory
of the man who courted me
with a clutch of gold richness cradled in his arms.
When he came through the front door
we rushed bedwards through my house,
night valley winds, the close trains rocking us long past ourselves
until he'd grope and find the hoard, peel and eat
and peel and feed me those home-grown globes.
We'd share the juicy whittle — the white lace of membranes
coating brown working hands, orange rime
across fingernails as we mixed sweat and sweet
into our sacrament.

Once again, I think. Let sun's nectar, time's sharp juice
pulse down my throat. Don't let me forget.

OTHERING

Once, I tried to imagine it —

not reading — nothing — not clouds, nor the inky residue
of night; not the pages of sheets rumpled at bedside;
not squirrels chattering on weathered fences,
responding to the inquisitions of winter; not
typescripts of age, skin of children tightening
into more serious play; not summer sun hurling out flames
until the day's hammocks melt into their seasonal plots;
not ever to enjoy the novelties of spring;

not sleeping — no singular cocoon of escape
while oceans and winds beat the planet out of perfect orbit;
no swimming deeper to grasp air bubbles of hope
and ride them to the surface; no clasp of sweaty terror
redeemed by daylight; never to enter the broadest texts
of stillness, to recount genealogies into darkness;
no begats or regrets; no blinding luck, no tomb, cave,
diurnal stone-tumbled renewal; no luck;

not eating — never coming sweetsour to one's senses
playing across the tongue; no luncheons on lawns
under canopy trees; no Italian terraces and cheese rinds
of nostril-fluting delicacy; no seeking, no Braille
of spice and salt, ocean-scent of body's luck; no reason
to stroke the belly, flat or convex; simply existing within
the absence of — ; no tides of flesh, green howls
of unrooting; no blame, no satiety, no animal ease;

not loving — fingers rude and blunt — mere digits, bland
instruments; not waiting or wanting; no breath of moon
in the ear of dawn; solitary and unaware of absence,
or absent and not missed; featherless, wings furled;

untouched by cataclysm; earthbound on an empty road; no attitude
toward sunset; chorus of frogs lost on infinite jet streams
where blue sky reclines, a lonely god; not made in anyone's image —
literate, impervious, dull; and rarely, if ever, heard from;

if other, so little then to make of life, of this, of life, this — this.

THE CANCER PATIENT
WRITES IN THE DARK

Look at my hands
trembling inside themselves
in the sparking of a luminous
clock face.
Three a.m., my fingers hold each other,
tight muscle, corded nerves,
skeins of them wound round bone.

I raise my hands to the moonlight,
stick straight pins
through translucent flesh into marrow,
testing if it is gone yet.

*

As I ease my bones
onto your body,
as I stiffen then soften,
so soften your bones.
Your wide eyes in the dark
lift off your pillow,
stare when I pour
this purging dream
and fill you like a cup of poison.

*

If awake in the dawn
I would admit it,
turn and say without sound,
  "I'm scared"
or tattoo with my finger

on your back while you sleep,
  "I'm finally dying,"
would you see it tomorrow,
pulling a shirt down snug to your waist?

*

A white carved fossil shakes
on your breast
the morning air
is a lungful of strength.
You kick leaves;
I saunter behind, without breath cry,
  "I'm dying, dying, dying."
Your feet kick,
responding, adamant,
  "Iknow Iknow Iknow."

THIS TIME

Afternoon
curls into a hedge of bright azaleas —
white, pink, purple —
the life flush at the under-edge of fingernails —
the blood blush beneath warm flesh —
the sensitive inside of eyelids
closed against light, for pure pleasure.
I'm waiting for evening
to unroll its velvety throat.
That's where the new moon waits,
her sly smile
lodged deep within a honey-stem of darkness.
I'm taking notes.
How carefully she rolls from new to full
and back again,
using all twenty-eight days to think things over.
This blue moon I won't be blue. This time,
I'm taking time,
so that it fills my arms
as hopefully as white blossoms
fill hawthorne's willing green hands.
It's almost too easy. So
I remember that too —
and promise to make my last moon
as round as a kiss
and as elegant as a calla lily,
But don't expect reverence.
A bit of a best friend, a bit of a bawd,
she and I plan to link arms along the way
and tell our tales. She will
drum blood through small ear canals
and leave me without breath on my last good day.

Until then, when I stand to soak in her bliss,
in the owls' waves of warm spring air she rides on,
take my measure by how much I give —
it's how much I'll make of this,
this time.

SKATING AND SLEIGHING
TO THE ICY VAULTS OF DEATH

It would be pleasant to choose the circumstances
of death. The relatives helping you to look ahead
and the children wondering where it is you will go.
Everything arranged in solemn chiaroscuro
as you die in climates that are gentle and well-known,
the family churchyard quiet as the leaves fall.
But always to die in bed with the weather at bay
and the chains of illness breaking as you prepare to leave!

Or exchange that dream for one of wintry lands,
become a peasant of the far Spreewald, a woman
as twisted as the roots that carvers pare to Christ's
dying in bands and thorns in the old stave church.
Your children mourn. Your best friends wipe flour
and lard from their hands to put on finery, frock coats,
silk hats, and thick embroidery on skirts and belts,
everyone crowds your room for messages from the shadowy
spheres that you disturb but you call out only blessings
when you expire. Your sleigh is decked with flowers of paper
and of cloth. In midwinter, the river thickens with ice.

Mourners glide you to your grave around each bend.
They skate you to an icy heaven and in ice you dwell.
The retreating sigh of skates your last breath,
It is impossible to arrange the circumstances of death.

MY IMPATIENCE

zombies me. I
         yearn,
xanthous and ill,
         withdraw convictions, create a personal
variorum of decisions
             undertaken, then undone.
Trillions of pre-dawn worries,
         sardonic and imprecise,
     rummage — wreak havoc — but do so
quietly. I, alone,
      precipitate my self-
obloquy, ruminating through every
      nook and cranial cavity. Dreams,
            mordant and
lofty, leave me excavating rueful
        kernels of desire.
Jejune possibilities infuriate; flywheels
              intervolve into stomach knots.
Hothouse hopes, like
        guerillas of nagging inactivity,
fracture opportunity into foolish bites. I
          estimate escapes and
dredge disasters.
     Cronied with wastefulness,
burglared of the here and now, I face such an

avalanche of nothing.

I LEARN TO STAND UP STRAIGHT

as if a May
Day pole were dropped
from javelin-height
and centered through me.
No more slumping to read
or bending wrong
to pick up lucky pennies.

My breath whooshes
into sudden openings
the way spring-warm dawn
enters the house
from a doorway.
I walk into morning
as my breath walks out of me —
leaving spleen, stomach,
kidneys, liver
to settle as they should.

I don't need to detail scars
although I could
for these days
specificity is taught —
hell, I teach it —
say to say, *purpled bruise*
from bike fall on right thigh,
say to say, *cauterize, ligature,
needle prick*, or *scalpel loss* —
but I don't.

What matters
centers around
two bone cages:

ribs that clasp heart
skull that holds

brain's electricity.
An expansive
bracelet of spine
links, spirals between,
to allow for bend and sway.
Every organ, muscle,
scar, cell, memory
takes up its proper place.

I step out mindfully this way.

DREAMS OF HOUSES

I remembered the house by day
And came to it again by night
When I began to dream.
Entering the door, I paused to survey
The rooms where I once lived.
I imagined the cat on a window ledge.
He slept overlooking the yard
And the sycamore tree and the grasses
Laced with seasonal leaves.
I bypassed the kitchen for the den
Where the heater worked ceaselessly
Against the rains. Old glass panes
Steamed and I would sit in the morning,
During storm weather, avoiding my work.

But the house was cold, the bookcases
Filled with someone else's books.
I looked at a dresser: perfumes,
Unstoppered, smelled of dust,
And dust coated strangers' pictures.
Everything was different
Yet I felt it was only days
Since I had left, since I last petted
The cat who never caught a blue jay
But was always in his way getting ready.
Memories can so fill a place
They are slow to disperse.
The house, though changed, waits for me
Whenever I return at night to rest.
So I closed the door carefully before I left.

ABOUT THE AUTHOR

Wendy Bishop, Ph.D., was a Kellogg W. Hunt distinguished professor of English at Florida State University. She was a highly respected teacher and internationally recognized researcher in the field of rhetoric and composition, as well as a widely published poet and literary author. She was the author and/or editor of 22 scholarly books and several poetry chapbooks, in addition to numerous articles and short stories. She was a much sought-after presenter and speaker at professional conferences. She served as chair of the Conference on College Composition and Communication and as a co-vice president and member of the board of directors for the Associated Writing Programs (AWP). She died in 2003.